NOW IT'S YOUR MOVE:
A Guide for the Outplaced Employee

FREDERICK W. DeROCHE

MARY A. McDOUGALL

Prentice-Hall, Inc., Englewood Cliffs, New Jersey 07632

Library of Congress Cataloging in Publication Data

DeRoche, Frederick W.
  Now it's your move.

  Includes index.
  1. Job hunting—Handbooks manuals, etc. I. McDougall,
Mary. II. Title.
HF5382.7.D47 1984   650.1'4   83–21257
ISBN 0-13-625434-9
ISBN 0-13-625426-8 (pbk.)

Editorial/production supervision and interior design: Fred Dahl
Cover design: Photo Plus Art, Celine Brandes
Manufacturing buyer: Ed O'Dougherty

Printed in the United States of America

10 9 8 7 6 5 4 3 2 1

ISBN 0-13-625434-9

ISBN 0-13-625426-8 {PBK.}

Prentice-Hall International, Inc., *London*
Prentice-Hall of Australia Pty. Limited, *Sydney*
Editora Prentice-Hall do Brasil, Ltda., *Rio de Janeiro*
Prentice-Hall Canada Inc., *Toronto*
Prentice-Hall of India Private Limited, *New Delhi*
Prentice-Hall of Japan, Inc., *Tokyo*
Prentice-Hall of Southeast Asia Pte. Ltd., *Singapore*
Whitehall Books Limited, *Wellington, New Zealand*

Contents

3

Assessment of career values and motives 23

4

Assessment of career skills 45

5

Life work planning: What are my options? 68

6

Relocating for a new job 94

11

Starting your next job on the right foot *203*

Foreword

One of the few good things to come out of the lamentable recession of 1981–1982 has been a whole new look at the process by which employers separate the people they must let go. In years past, the process was simple, quick, and often cruel. Higher management prepared a list, and on the final payday each person received word about their severance in the form of a pink slip inserted in his or her paycheck. The stress of separation was aggravated by the shock of abruptness and curt notification.

A few firms in those industries that were first hit by the need to trim their work force did the sad deed more professionally, with some advance preparation. While many such programs were internal to the firms, they attracted the attention of a number of consultants and behavioral scientists, such as Fred DeRoche and Mary McDougall.

Their research and work in outplacement led them to the principal features of such programs. The results of that research and their experience as practicing consultants are contained in this book.

Structured outplacement assistance comprises a new development in human resources management, which will last long after the presently painful depression is gone and, we hope, forgotten.

Mary and Fred have defined clearly the essential elements of "outplacement." The basic premise is to ease the psychological and social stress that attends being "dehired," and then to assist employees to move on with their careers.

The whole process is now more professional and humane than it used to be, in no small part because of the important study and practice the authors of this book have presented. In large firms with hundreds of layoffs, where the job is managed by a full-time staff of professionals and even where individuals are few in number, the professional personnel manager (now usually called the Human Resources Manager) will be able to apply what is eminently common sense in an organized and systematic fashion by a reading of this work.

The book presents an organized and intelligently planned outplacement approach, which can benefit the company and the employee.

As President Truman learned from his experience with the relief of General MacArthur, people at large have strong feelings that "the act may be necessary, but there is a right way and a wrong way to do it."

From the employee viewpoint, the book provides a way to protect people's self-esteem, help them mount a job search campaign, assist in resume planning and financial organization, consider every retirement option, and work out their frustration and sense of alienation which inevitably comes from separation. Stress often comes from traumatic separations, we are told, and this book makes one of life's most traumatic experiences more humane, sensible, and orderly.

GEORGE S. ODIORNE
Amherst, Massachusetts

Introduction

Today, many people are being outplaced, caught up in economic workforce reductions, considering career changes, looking for new jobs, planning for retirement, plateaued in their jobs, or just working in deadend situations. If you find yourself in any of these situations, then this book can help you clarify and work out your next career move. The underlying principle of the book is that most people improve their job or life situations when they utilize a structured decision-making process. In fact, one recent study showed that 71 percent of terminated managerial employees were earning more in their new jobs than they had previously earned.

The book requires two things of you. First, you should spend a considerable amount of time and energy working with this book. While we can't guarantee you a job, we can help you increase your chances for successful reemployment in less time. Second, have your spouse or a close friend agree to work through the book with you or to discuss sections of it. It's best to hear yourself talk out some of these concerns. We also suggest joining structured support groups, such as job clubs, to help you follow through on your career goals.

The book is a "work" book. It is a "work" book because job hunting is very demanding work—requiring your full-time efforts and energy. It is a "work" book because it obliges you to write, talk, and think. Working through a section of the book at a time is more appropriate than reading the entire book all at once. When finished, you should have done much writing. In our personal counseling, we require clients to do plenty of "homework" because we know writing can be a clarifying experience. This homework gives you a clear picture of who you are, what you want, and what you will say to prospective employers.

We have written this book in a conversational style that is suitable to a counseling framework. The book has short chapters. You may not need all of them, but we have tried to cover as many outplacement strategies as possible. For example, if you are not planning to retire soon, you may not spend much time with Chapter 7. If you are retiring and considering a second career, you may find Chapters 3 and 4 helpful. You may not need Chapter 8 if you are not a dual-career family. Or, if you have decided not to relocate, Chapter 6 can be skimmed.

Finally, we strongly recommend that you work your way through the workbook in the order outlined. The sequence is arranged to cover the issues as they are usually experienced. We wish you every success as you grow in your new career.

FRED DeROCHE AND MARY McDOUGALL

Acknowledgments

This book is an integration of many views and theories. We have been influenced by our individual and corporate clients and acknowledge their contribution to our learning and professional development.

Of all the persons who have contributed to this book, we particularly want to acknowledge the support and encouragement of Jack Bologna, Jeanne Knopf DeRoche, Tom McDougall, Gerald Reilly, and Barbara Davis who typed the manuscript.

1

Coping with your unemployment period

Unemployment is an emotionally confusing time. You may feel angry, depressed, scared, ill, and relieved all at the same time. You may be unable to think clearly and feel a personal inner void.

Having these feelings is quite normal. More than likely, you did not expect to be fired, laid off, or outplaced. Healthy, well-adjusted people become frightened, angry, and upset when they have to deal with unexpected changes in their lives. Your life probably had a routine, in which you and your family felt secure. This new feeling of insecurity is personally disorienting to you, as well as to your spouse and family.

You may also experience a sense of failure and rejection. "Why is this happening to me?" If you have worked for a company for many years and now have been told that you are no longer needed, that sense of belonging turns into a sense of rejection from the group. This rejection can be a real blow to your self-worth.

Because our self-respect is too often measured by where we work, you may have problems socializing. You may find it difficult to tell your friends, neighbors, or club members that you are unemployed. "What will they think?" So you might cover up these issues with evasions. Other fears stem from income loss and financial insecurity. Awareness of continuing family expenses intensifies these fears. Accordingly, research has shown that the emotional impact of termination is more severe if it causes major changes in social and economic status due to the firing or layoff. Also, if you are feeling personally guilty over the job loss, your anxiety may be greater.

THE TERMINATION/REEMPLOYMENT PROCESS*

The emotional reactions experienced by job loss are not unlike the grief associated with the death of a spouse, parent, or child. From the theories articulated by Granger Westberg and Elizabeth Kubler-Ross, we know that people experiencing a sense of loss normally move through a series of distinct emotional reactions or stages. Similarly, University of Michigan sociologist, Louis Ferman, has identified major trauma points in the unemployment/reemployment cycle. The trauma points occur during the pre-job loss period, at the actual job termination, upon the exhausting of benefits, during the intensive job search, and when adjusting to a new job.

The unemployment "crisis" can initiate a personal change. The Chinese have long been aware of the connection

*This section is based on Robert B. Garber, "The Psychology of Termination and Outplacement," in *Employment Termination Handbook, Legal and Psychological Guidelines for Employers.* New York: Executive Enterprises Publications Co., Inc., 1981.

FIGURE 1–1

TERMINATION/REEMPLOYMENT PROCESS

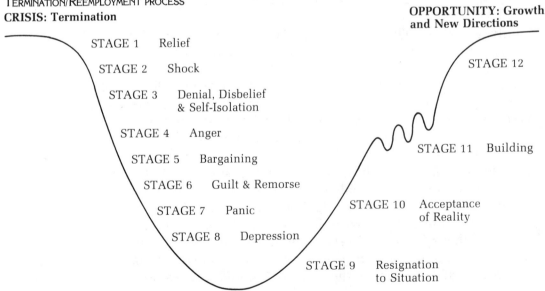

CRISIS: Termination

OPPORTUNITY: Growth and New Directions

STAGE 1 Relief

STAGE 2 Shock

STAGE 12

STAGE 3 Denial, Disbelief & Self-Isolation

STAGE 4 Anger

STAGE 5 Bargaining

STAGE 11 Building

STAGE 6 Guilt & Remorse

STAGE 7 Panic

STAGE 10 Acceptance of Reality

STAGE 8 Depression

STAGE 9 Resignation to Situation

COPING WITH YOUR UNEMPLOYMENT

between crises and change. The Chinese term for "crisis"— *wei-ji*—is composed of the characters for "danger" and "opportunity." The concepts of Westberg, Kubler-Ross, Ferman, and the cultural view of the Chinese form the bases of the *Termination/Reemployment Process*. This sequential, developmental process is brought on by the "crisis" of unemployment. (See Figure 1–1.)

Regardless of how you become unemployed—fired, laidoff, caught in a plant slowdown or workforce reduction, a job change, even if voluntary—you can go through these stages as a result of "grieving" the loss of something very important—your job. In most cases, you experience this process one stage at a time and usually do not skip stages. The sequence may vary, and stages may overlap. Feelings of shock, disbelief, denial, and anger can be experienced simultaneously. However, seldom are the acceptance and accomodation stages reached until denial, anger, bargaining, guilt, panic, and depression have been experienced. Let's consider a further description of each stage.

1. *Relief*. People react to the news of termination or layoff in various ways. Some people actually experience a sense of relief at the news. With substantial unemployment benefits and severance packages, former employees often make the assumption that they're on an extended vacation and thus delay dealing with the reality of their unemployment.

2. *Shock*. Others may feel numb when they first receive the news of their termination or layoff. This sense of shock may be felt more severely if the termination is not expected.

3. *Denial, Disbelief, and Self-Isolation*. You do not believe that you have been let go or terminated. Often you do not want to talk about your termination with your family and friends. You may even lie about your dismissal or layoff. You may find yourself in a "flight" situation, feeling as though you're moving about in a daze for some time. Short-term denial is a healthy way of dealing with the uncomfortable and painful situation, and it helps people to collect themselves after unexpected shocking news.

4. *Anger*. When denial cannot be maintained any longer, the person may experience feelings of anger, envy, resentment. This is usually in response to personal questions like,

"Why me? . . . It should have been him." You may begin to displace your anger by attacking your former company, your boss, fellow workers, employed workers in general, your spouse and children. You blame them for your termination. You're in a "fighting" situation.

5. *Bargaining*. You may look for other alternatives to postpone the inevitable. You may try to have your employment situation reconsidered, even knowing that there is little or no chance of being reinstated. You may propose alternative solutions to your former employer for the possibility of rehiring you.

6. *Guilt and Remorse*. Sometimes the bargaining comes from feeling guilty and remorseful that perhaps you did not do your job well. You begin to blame yourself for the termination due to your past job performance. When unemployment is extended over a long period, guilt feelings may be intensified by not fulfilling the "provider" role when the family begins to do without. A sense of failure is dominant.

7. *Panic*. You begin with a flurry of frenzied job search activities. You may spend hours reading want ads but not apply for jobs. You try to get interviews for jobs for which you do not qualify. You rush out to interviews without being prepared. From this sporadic, disorganized activity, you assume that there are no jobs.

8. *Depression*. This stage of unemployment is usually inevitable. Experiencing a loss of self-identity, security, independence, and self-esteem, you have very little control over your life situations. You begin to sleep more or less, eat more or less, drink more or less. Marital and family communication problems begin to occur or intensify. Among men, sexual impotence is common. The spouse and family may view unemployment as a sign of laziness. The spouse and children may also begin to experience symptoms of stress, with the children having problems at school. Usually you find it very difficult to think of talking to prospective employers. Also, there is often a short period of idealization—of looking back and believing that everything was perfect before and wishing to "just go back there again."

9. *Resignation to Situation*. Acceptance and accomodation begin with resigning yourself to the facts that you are

unemployed and that you will not be working for your previous employer. You begin to accept those facts and realize that you must do something about them, even though you may still feel resentful, angry, guilty, depressed.

10. *Acceptance of Reality*. Recovery, which leads to growth and new directions, comes only after the resolution of the preceding stages. You begin to see your potential and to develop goals and expectations for the future. You now can make constructive plans to change yourself and your situation. This time is generally the best to begin an intensive career assessment and job search. However, a long job search campaign and rejection from prospective employers can trigger temporary relapses to any of the previous stages.

11. *Building*. This stage usually begins with making a major decision about your future. The decision may be to accept a new job, to complete your education, to train for a new occupation, to retire, or to pursue a combination of these possibilities. Adjusting to the new situation inevitably causes some stress and anxiety. The job may pay less, be lower-status, or have fewer benefits, which necessitates adjustment to a new lifestyle. A decision to work and return to school requires major adjustments in the family schedule and budget. A retirement decision involves a whole new lifestyle. Even though family members may say that they support you in your new situation, they may not like the adjustments forced upon them by your new schedule, and they may wish that things could go back to "normal." Dealing with such resistance finds you second-guessing your decisions, even though you are progressing in terms of your own goals.

12. *Growth and New Directions*. Formerly unemployed persons often say in hindsight, "It was the best thing that could have happened to me. I would never have done this myself. I was too safe and secure. But this forced me to see what else I could do and I'm happy for it now." Most personal growth and development is precipitated by a crisis, and most of us do not voluntarily put ourselves in a crisis situation. However, when forced to move in new directions, we generally become stronger and happier persons.

An important aspect of this process is the length of time that people take to move through the entire cycle. Research indicates that there is a high correlation between the length of time necessary to resolve each stage and the importance of the loss in your life. If you had been working for a company for 25 to 30 years with strong personal feelings of identification, you are likely to grieve longer than if you had been there for only a year or two. For shorter periods of employment, you may have minimal emotional reactions to the loss immediately after termination or layoff. When the unemployment period becomes extensive, you may experience a delayed emotional reaction.

Everyone needs time to work through grieving, self-pity, and guilt. While one person can do so in a week or two, others may need more time. You may feel you have worked through most of these issues and then be surprised when they emerge again during your job search campaign. Remember, you are accommodating yourself to a new situation. These feelings have not been completely eradicated, but often just replaced with new concerns. Usually, it is difficult to begin a fruitful self-assessment process and intensive marketing campaign until you have worked through the peak of these grieving emotions. Beginning an active job search is often a way of moving on into the Accepting/Accommodation stages.

MY REACTION TO TERMINATION

Directly after being terminated, you may isolate yourself and deny what has happened to you. It is important to identify your emotional reactions and to realize that these reactions are healthy and normal. Denying these feelings and refusing to talk about them may inhibit your adjustment and ability to conduct a positive job campaign. In a few weeks you may have to answer an interviewer's questions about why you were fired, how you would describe your last boss, or what you disliked about your previous employer. If you haven't confronted and talked openly about your emotional reaction, it will be difficult to do so with the interviewer.

Work through these exercises with your spouse or someone close to you. During this unemployment period, you need emotional support from your family and friends. If spouses and friends are to offer emotional support, they need to identify and understand your feelings. In a study conducted over a two-year period, the physical and emotional consequences of involuntary job loss were examined in one hundred married men laid off in two plant shutdowns. Those in rural areas enjoyed a significantly higher level of social support from wife, relatives, and friends than those in urban areas. The less supported men showed significantly higher levels of cholesterol, symptoms of illness, and negative emotional responses.

Before reading on to the next section of the chapter, complete the questionnaire in Exercise 1–1 and have your spouse/friend complete the one in Exercise 1–2. Then discuss your reactions, using questions in Exercise 1–3.

EXERCISE 1–1: SELF

Instructions

As a result of your recent termination, you may be experiencing the emotions in the following list. Study the list.

Self-pity	Hatred	Fright
Defeat	Contentment	Worthlessness
Anger	Rejection	Guilt
Puzzlement	Disorientation	Depression
Resentment	Self-confidence	Accepting
Denial	Devastation	Abandoned
Fear of future	Trauma	Hopeful
Shock	Anxiety	Frustrated
Listlessness	Nausea	My life's falling apart

Now do the following:

1. Identify the emotions you experience most often, and write them in Column 1.
2. In Column 2, rank the items from Column 1 by putting the most important item in space #1 and continuing until #6.
3. Identify the emotions that you think your spouse or close friend is experiencing regarding your recent termination. Write them in Column #3.

4. In Column 4, rank the items from Column 3 by putting what you think is the most important one of your spouse's feelings in space #1 and continuing until #6.

5. After you and your spouse or close friend have completed the first four columns, get together for an hour to discuss what you have written. Begin by copying your spouse's responses from his or her Columns 3 and 4 and writing that in your Columns 5 and 6. Then have your spouse record your responses from your Columns 3 and 4, and write them into his or her Columns 5 and 6.

Column 1	*Column 3*	*Column 5*
————	————	————
————	————	————
————	————	————
————	————	————
————	————	————
————	————	————

Column 2	*Column 4*	*Column 6*
1 ————	1 ————	1 ————
2 ————	2 ————	2 ————
3 ————	3 ————	3 ————
4 ————	4 ————	4 ————
5 ————	5 ————	5 ————
6 ————	6 ————	6 ————

EXERCISE 1–2: SPOUSE / FRIEND

Instructions

As a result of your spouse's or close friend's recent termination, you may have been experiencing the feelings in the following list. Study the list.

Anger	Hatred	Fright
Self-pity	Contentment	Worthlessness
Defeat	Rejection	Guilt
Puzzlement	Disorientation	Depressed
Resentment	Self-confidence	Accepting
Denial	Devastation	Abandoned
Fear of future	Trauma	Hopeful
Shock	Anxiety	Frustrated
Listlessness	Nausea	My life's falling apart

Now do the following.

1. Identify the emotions you experience most often, and write them in Column 1.
2. In Column 2, rank the items from Column 1 by putting the most important item in space #1 and continuing until #6.
3. Identify the emotions that you think your spouse or close friend is experiencing regarding his or her recent termination, and write them in Column #3.
4. In Column 4, rank the items from Column 3 by putting what you think is the most important one of your spouse's or friend's feelings in space #1 and continue until #6.
5. After you and your spouse/close friend have completed the first four columns, get together for an hour to discuss what you have written. Begin by copying your spouse's/friend's responses from his/her Column 3 and 4. Then write them in Columns 5 and 6. Next have your spouse/friend record your responses from your Columns 3 and 4, and write them in his/her Column 5 and 6.

Column 1	Column 3	Column 5
_____	_____	_____
_____	_____	_____
_____	_____	_____
_____	_____	_____
_____	_____	_____
_____	_____	_____

Column 2	Column 4	Column 6
1 _____	1 _____	1 _____
2 _____	2 _____	2 _____
3 _____	3 _____	3 _____
4 _____	4 _____	4 _____
5 _____	5 _____	5 _____
6 _____	6 _____	6 _____

EXERCISE 1–3:
ISSUES FOR DISCUSSION AND ACTION

Instructions

Put an **X** on the line where it accurately indicates your response to each of questions 1–4.

1. How easy [How difficult] was it for you to identify and prioritize your current feelings?

   _____

   Very Easy   Very Difficult

2. How easy [How difficult] was it for you to identify the emotions you think your spouse/friend is currently feeling?

   _____

   Very Easy   Very Difficult

3. How accurate were you in knowing your spouse's/friend's reactions?

   _____

   Extremely Accurate   Extremely Inaccurate

4. How accurate was your spouse/friend in knowing your emotional reactions?

   _____

   Extremely Accurate   Extremely Inaccurate

5. What specific actions can each of you do to emotionally support one another?

- _____
- _____
- _____
- _____
- _____
- _____

CONTROLLING YOUR STRESS

Stress is the feeling that our bodies experience when reacting biochemically to new demands. In adapting to life's disruptions and imbalances, we experience physiological changes in form of faster heart rate, increased respiration, higher blood pressure, and changes in body temperature. Your involuntary termination therefore puts you into an inherently stressful situation because you are dealing with new demands.

The extent of your reaction to unemployment depends on your ability to tolerate stress. Individuals react to changes in their environment in various ways, and their responses may even vary at different times in their lives. If you are either in a two-career family or in a mature stage of your career, you may respond more stressfully than if you are planning for retirement. Each time you experience stress, your body needs time to adapt and restore its equilibrium. If the length of your unemployment is extremely long, or if you have other personal problems in addition to seeking a job, at times you may exceed your threshold or tolerance level. Your resources for fighting stress may become depleted, and your body is signaling that it just can't take anymore.

When you are unemployed, consider using your stress as an energizing force. Robert Kreitner, in his article, "Managing the Two Faces of Stress," reports that whether stress is energizing or destructive depends on two dimensions. The first is frequency—how often we encounter stress-producing situations or events. The second is the magnitude of the stress— how intensely we respond to potentially stressful events.

When we experience stress frequently or respond to it too intensely, we are entering a danger zone, and stress becomes potentially destructive. For example, an individual who has not learned to manage stress is the person who responds violently to infrequent stress. Another such individual is the "slow burner"—the person who continually absorbs stress but who does not respond until the accumulation becomes unmanageable and explosive.

Stress can therefore be either energizing or debilitating. Consider how it affects our behavior. If no demands were placed on us, no stimulation to act on, we would accomplish nothing. Up to a point, then, stress enhances behavior by activating us. Beyond this point, our behavior decreases due to too much stress. The point of tolerance is different for everyone, and to understand how we reach our personal tolerance level, we need to understand the causes of stress. For example, if your firing was a total surprise to you, it may be more stressful than if you had anticipated it. If you had little or no control over the situation, you cannot make choices about how you are going to adapt. If your job meant everything to you, you will feel more stress than if you were personally planning on leaving the organization and your past employer simply assisted your efforts.

In planning for your transition, it is important to predict what will happen to you and your family so you can take steps to prepare. Preparation doesn't make this time free of stress for you and your family, but it can minimize the amount of stress that you experience.

EXERCISE 1–4: CONTROLLING YOUR TIME

Many unemployed people mismanage their time. Those who practice time management on the job don't always transfer their methods to nonwork situations. Now they find they get very little accomplished. Alan Lakein in his book, *How to Get Control of Your Time and Your Life*, says that you have to learn how to plan what you want to do and then organize your use of time to get it done. Time is a constant that you cannot change; you can only control your own behavior with respect to time.

Instructions

The first step in planning how to manage your time is to assess how you currently use your time.

1. Figure 1–2 is an inventory of your daily life—how you *actually* spend your time and energy. Estimate the number of hours you spend in your day on the following categories. Then draw slices in the pie to proportionately represent each category.

- Sleeping
- Eating
- Food preparation
- Job search
- Television

- Exercise
- Work (full- or part-time)
- Reading
- Yard maintenance
- Travel

- House maintenance
- Hobbies/games
- Friends/socializing
- Family socializing
- Shopping

FIGURE 1–2
DAILY LIFE SCHEDULE

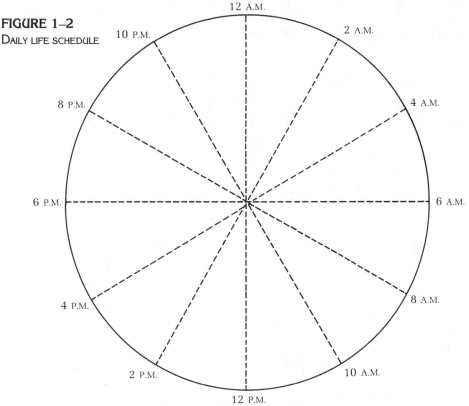

Reprinted by permission of A&W Publishers, Inc. from *Values Clarification: A Handbook of Practical Strategies for Teachers and Students,* New Revised Edition, by Sidney B. Simon, Leland W. Howe, and Howard Kirschenbaum. Copyright © 1972; copyright © 1978. Hart Publishing Company, Inc.

2. Figure 1–3 is an inventory of your daily life—how you
   would like to spend your time and energy. Then draw
   slices in the pie to proportionately represent each category. Use the same list of categories.

FIGURE 1–3

<small>PREFERRED DAILY SCHEDULE</small>

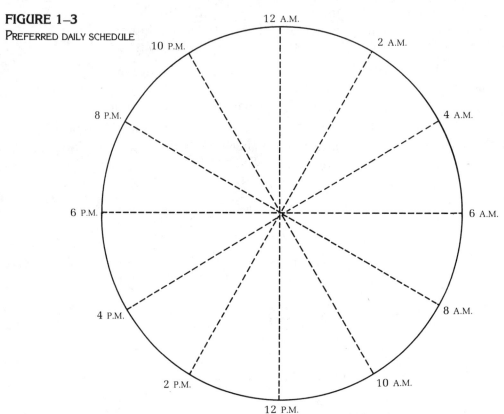

Reprinted by permission of A&W Publishers, Inc. from *Values Clarifi-*
cation: A Handbook of Practical Strategies for Teachers and Students, New
Revised Edition, by Sidney B. Simon, Leland W. Howe, and Howard
Kirschenbaum. Copyright © 1972; copyright © 1978. Hart Publishing Company, Inc.

3. When you have completed Figures 1–2 and 1–3, answer
   the following questions: What gaps exist between your
   Daily Schedule and your Preferred Schedule?

   _____

   _____

   _____

   _____

4. After you have examined the gaps or imbalances between the two schedules, you should identify your goals and then prioritize them. What do you want to accomplish? For example, during this transition period from one employment situation to another, you obviously want to get another job—that's the entire purpose of outplacement. But what else? Perhaps you want to analyze and assess yourself, along with your direction. Maybe you want to travel, take a vacation, remodel the kitchen, paint the house, or plan your retirement. You may have a number of goals related or unrelated to getting another position.

Identify the major goals that you want to accomplish in the next two or three months. List them in the left-hand column marked "Goals."

Goals	*Priority*
_____	_____
_____	_____
_____	_____
_____	_____
_____	_____
_____	_____
_____	_____

5. Once you have identified what you want to accomplish, evaluate what is very important and what is not so important. On the right-hand side, in the column marked "Priority," rate each goal according to the following scale:

A = Top Priority, Most Important
B = Less Important Goals
C = Low Priority Goals

With a sense of your goals and their priority, you can anticipate how you will manage your time during your employment transition period. You can build a schedule of activities around accomplishing your "A" goals. Perhaps you don't have to spend all your time on them, but you will spend the necessary time to achieve these top priorities. The question is, How can you change your daily schedule to do the things you most want to do and live more the way you wish? List specific actions in the left-hand column, along with the dates that you will begin to do them in the right-hand column.

Action Plan   *Dates*

_____   _____

_____   _____

_____   _____

_____   _____

_____   _____

_____   _____

_____   _____

_____   _____

_____   _____

_____   _____

_____   _____

_____   _____

References for Further Reading

Ferman, Louis A. "After the Shutdown: The Social and Psychological Consequences of Job Displacement," *ILR Report* (Spring 1981), pp. 22–26.

Hall, Francine, S. and Douglas T. Hall. *The Two Career Couple.* Reading, Mass.: Addison-Wesley Publishing Company, 1979.

Holmes, T. H.. & R. H. Rahe. "The Social Readjustment Rating Scale," *Journal of Psychosomatic Research*, 11 (1967) Pergamon Press, Ltd.

Kreitner, Robert. "Managing the Two Faces of Stress," *Arizona Business* (October 1977), pp. 9–14.

Kubler-Ross, Elizabeth. *On Death and Dying.* New York: MacMillan Publishing Company, 1979.

Lakein, Alan. *How to Get Control of Your Time and Your Life.* New York: Wyden, 1973.

McLean, Alan A., M.A. *Work Stress.* Reading, Mass.: Addison-Wesley Publishing Company, 1979.

Westburg, Granger E. *Good Grief.* Rock Island, Illinois: Augustana Book Concern, 1961.

2

Personal financial planning

When you are facing your unemployment situation realistically, one of the first reactions you may have is the fearful and frightening thought, "How will I manage financially? . . . How will I keep my creditors from repossessing my house, my car, the things that I need?" Handling the financial situation in a straightforward and productive manner can be difficult. When caught in a financial squeeze, intelligent people often do not rationally think through their options. Addressing financial matters in a very practical way, you can begin to take control of your situation. Working through the Financial Planning Exercise in Figure 2–1 enables you to develop a working cash flow budget, which can sustain you and your family during the unemployment period.

Be realistic when estimating the length of your unemployment period. For some persons, a year or more is not an unrealistic period of time to locate new employment, while others may reestablish themselves in a matter of weeks.

EXERCISE 2–1: FINANCIAL PLANNING

Instructions

1. To complete the Cash Flow Budget in Table 2–1, review payroll stubs, unemployment insurance receipts, severance pay, stock dividends, and other sources of income.

(Unemployment insurance is taxable.) Be sure to include any sources of cash income from supplemental jobs.

2. To complete the expense section, review the past six months' financial records, checkbook entries, and monthly invoices. Asterisked items may be annual or semi-annual payments, depending on your personal payment structure. So it is essential that the total amount appears in Column 3 whether or not they are itemized monthly. To calculate Column 3, estimate the number of months that you anticipate being unemployed, and then multiply Column 2 by that number of months and complete Column 3.

3. The net effect is to ascertain whether you will be in a financial deficit situation at the end of your projected unemployment period. Filling out the Analysis of Your Projected Budget (Figure 2–1) enables you to make this determination. If the difference is negative, you have a deficit budget that requires additional action on your part. The following questions may help in determining possible courses of action.

TABLE 2–1

CASH FLOW BUDGET

		INCOME			
Line No.	Current Monthly Income			Transition Period Income	Total for Projected Unemployment Period
1. Salary	_____	Severance pay		_____	_____
2. Spouse's salary	_____	Unemployment		_____	_____
3. Other	_____	Salary		_____	_____
4. _____	_____	Other:			
5. _____	_____	Life insurance		_____	_____
6. _____	_____	Savings		_____	_____
7. _____	_____	Stocks		_____	_____
8. Total Monthly Income	_____			_____	_____

EXPENSES

Line No.	Fixed Expenses	Column 1: Current Monthly Expenses	Column 2: Transition Period Monthly Expenses	Column 3: Total for Projected Unemployment Period
9.	Mortgage/rent	_____	_____	_____
10.	Property taxes	_____	_____	_____
11.	Life Insurance	_____	_____	_____
12.	Auto(s)	_____	_____	_____
13.	Auto	_____	_____	_____
14.	Auto insurance	_____	_____	_____
15.	Health insurance	_____	_____	_____
16.	Tuition	_____	_____	_____
17.	*Monthly charge Payments	_____	_____	_____
18.	Telephone	_____	_____	_____
19.	Electricity	_____	_____	_____
20.	Gas/Oil (heating)	_____	_____	_____
21.	Water	_____	_____	_____
22.	Medical/drugs	_____	_____	_____
23.	Garbage disposal Service	_____	_____	_____
24.	Home maintenance	_____	_____	_____

Nonfixed Expenses

Line No.		Column 1	Column 2	Column 3
25.	Food	_____	_____	_____
26.	Gasoline	_____	_____	_____
27.	Auto maintenance	_____	_____	_____
28.	Contributions	_____	_____	_____
29.	Entertainment	_____	_____	_____
30.	Newspaper/magazines	_____	_____	_____
31.	Vacation	_____	_____	_____

TABLE 2–1
(Cont.)

	Monthly Charge Payments		
17a. Visa	_____	_____	_____
17b. Master Card	_____	_____	_____
17c. American Express	_____	_____	_____
17d. Carte Blanche	_____	_____	_____
17e. Diner's Club	_____	_____	_____
17f. Department Stores	_____	_____	_____
17g.	_____	_____	_____
17h.	_____	_____	_____
17i.	_____	_____	_____
17j. Other:	_____	_____	_____
17k. _____	_____	_____	_____
17l. _____	_____	_____	_____
32. Total Expenses	_____	_____	_____

FIGURE 2–1
ANALYSIS OF YOUR PROJECTED BUDGET

Total Projected Income for Unemployment Period (line 8 from Column 3)	$_____
Total Projected Expenses for Unemployment Period (line 32 from Column 3)	$_____
Subtract to find the difference	$_____

- What income sources do you have that can be readily converted to cash? (Consider stocks, bonds, other securities, late model automobiles, a summer home, the cash value of life insurance.)
- Which nonfixed expense items can be eliminated, modified, or postponed? (Consider vacations, entertainment, travel, major household appliances or furniture purchases, and special extra food items.)

- Which fixed expense items may be eliminated, postponed, or modified? (Consider insurance coverage, less costly educational alternatives, or second or third automobiles.)

Actions I Must Take   *By What Date*

_____   _____

_____   _____

_____   _____

_____   _____

_____   _____

_____   _____

FINANCIAL PLANNING

A major reason for financial planning during an unemployment period is to protect your credit rating while your income is reduced. If you find that your budget does not balance—that is, you do not have enough monthly income to pay your expenses—then consider a number of options:

1. Involve other family members in making decisions to deal with this family problem. Cooperation makes the plan more likely to work.
2. Establish priorities for making decisions about who gets paid first, second, and third. Top priority should be given to the creditors that have the greatest effect on the health and security of your family. For most people, the priorities are: house, utilities, seeking another job, car, and insurances. After these items, the next are debts to creditors with security. Can cars, appliances or other items be repossessed? Third in priority are debts in which you have built up a significant equity. If you have only a few payments left on an item, it may take preference. Fourth, look at first paying off debts with high interest rates. Generally, this sort of debt means credit cards since many of them can charge as high as 20.4 percent in interest a year.

3. After you establish your financial plan, you should contact the customer service representatives at the financial institutions or companies that service your accounts. Many banks, savings and loans, credit unions, finance or mortgage companies, retail firms, and utility companies have financial counselors or service representatives who are willing to work with you on alternative arrangements or reduced payments during the unemployment period. However, it is most important that you make contact immediately. By law, lending institutions must have minimum payments on loans within 45 to 60 days, or your account may be in default.

4. If you have problems making your new budget work, another option is to contact a credit couseling firm for assistance. However, beware of the cost involved. In most cases, they take a percentage of the total amount you owe (a minimum of 10 percent) as their service fee. They then contact your creditors and make arrangements for you. Usually, you turn over all your monthly income to the counselor, receive a fixed amount to live on, and the counselor pays your bills. Remember, you are incurring another expense by using this method. Self-discipline in this temporary period may be your best strategy.

5. Check your state social service agencies for government assistance programs for which you qualify.

References for Further Reading

May, John. *The RIF Survival Book: How to Manage Your Money if You're Unemployed*. Philadelphia, Pa.: Chilton Press, 1982.

Porter, Sylvia. *New Money Book for the 80's*. New York: Avon, 1980.

Quinn, Jane B. *Everyone's Money Book*. New York: Dell, 1980.

Van Castel, Venita. *Money Dynamics for the 1980's*. Reston, Va.: Reston Publishing Co., 1980.

3

Assessment of
career values and motives

Picture yourself sitting in a job interview right now. How prepared are you to thoroughly answer the interviewer's questions?

- What are your future career goals?
- Tell me some significant aspects of your career.
- What are three or five words that most aptly describe you?
- What would you say is the major motivating force or factor in your career development to date?

Can you control the situation by responding with complete statements that describe salable aspects of your background? Or would your response consist of a few stammered words—or, worse yet, complete silence? . . .

Successful reemployment is an integration of two processes:

1. the self-assessment of the outplaced employee, called the Career Identification Process (or "knowing yourself"), and
2. the Job Market Assessment, which can be called the person-job matching process.

These two processes are integrated in an Individual's Market Campaign Plan process, as outlined in Figure 3–1. In this chapter, you analyze your values, attitudes, and motives. In Chapter 4, you will identify your skills and competencies. Chapter 5 will help you to formulate this self-information into an Individual Marketing Plan with specific life and career goals.

From a time sequence, it is difficult to develop an individual Market Campaign Plan without first completing the Career Identification Process. This process, however, is never totally completed or finished. When you begin to move into the marketing phase, you may learn more about your values, skills, or goals, which may force you to update this self-knowledge.

As someone who was recently forced into the job market, you may not be prepared for interviewing because you may not have been in the job market for years. To thoroughly prepare for your market campaign, you need to spend time in self-assessment. Effective salespersons know their product lines thoroughly. As your own salesperson in your market campaign, the first rule is to "know yourself." It's your move. Your responsibility is to become as knowledgeable about yourself as you can, so you can promote yourself effectively.

Another key reason for spending a great deal of time working through these chapters is that self-assessment is an

FIGURE 3–1

REEMPLOYMENT PROCESS

OUTPLACED EMPLOYEE SELF-ASSESSMENT		JOB MARKET ASSESSMENT

CAREER ASSESSMENT OF

- Values
- Motives
- Skills
- Employment History
- Personal and Professional Goals

INDIVIDUAL MARKETING PLAN

POSITION REQUIREMENTS

- Tasks to be accomplished
- Desired levels of compentency
- Personality mesh

Rule 1:
KNOW YOURSELF

Rule 2:
KNOW YOUR JOB MARKET

exploration for new career opportunities. Maybe now is the right time for you to make a career change. Have you found that you were staying with your job or your employer mainly for security reasons? Maybe you no longer have your original interest and enthusiasm. Maybe you've been thinking for years that you wanted to explore other career options but never wanted to put the status quo at risk. Now may be your opportunity.

Before jumping blindly into something, however, it's best to do some thorough self-research. You must assess your skills, attitudes, and values to insure a significant mesh or fit between you and new opportunities.

Stand in front of a full-length mirror and look at yourself. Do you really know who you are? Can you identify your values, priorities, goals, interests, skills, competencies, successes, and achievements? Self-assessment, a process for developing and organizing yourself, is basic to planning and controlling your life and career. It is essential to all aspects of successful job-hunting. Knowing yourself affects which section of the job market you decide to explore, the way you present yourself on a resume, and your ability to be persuasive during an interview.

Many people decide their life work backwards. They choose first a career field and then a job in the field. Only then do they check into the skills needed on the job and proceed to obtain those skills. In this sequence, people are not relating their own assets to the job market. Look at Figure 3–2a. People normally start at the top of the chart and work down.

We suggest just the opposite approach as illustrated in Figure 3–2b. The black vertical line in Figure 3–2b indicates an integration of a series of personal choices from each of the major categories. To have a personally rewarding and satisfying career, begin at the bottom of the chart and assess your skills (S), values (V), and motives (M). After assessing these skills, values, and motives, you cluster, group, and organize them. How you go about doing so largely determines what you expect from your role, job, work environment, and career field. If the outcome of your personal choices (chosen field, work environment, job and role expectations) are greater or equal to what you originally expected or anticipated, then you can assume that your career will be satisfying.

FIGURE 3–2
CONTEXT OF SATISFYING CAREER

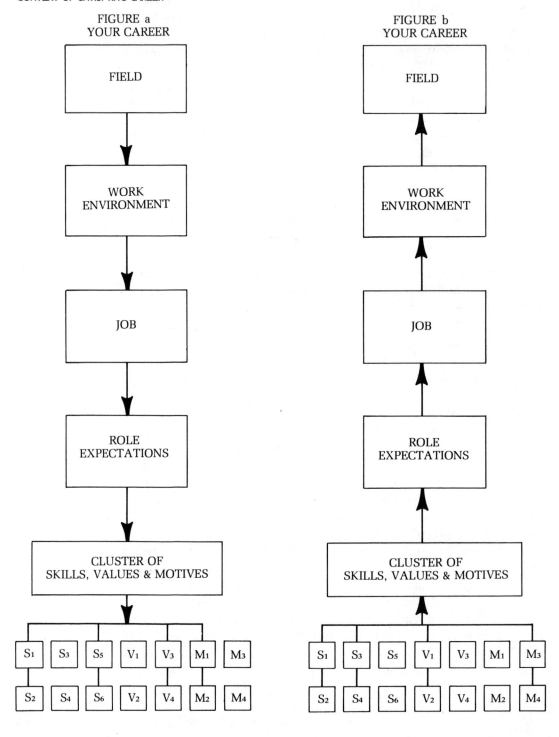

From this outline, you can see that you have to analyze and assess many variables in your career before you begin to investigate the job market. With this assessment process, you gain an increased self-awareness and a clearer understanding of yourself—both critical to the personal marketing process that follows.

You have to periodically reassess your skills, values, and motives, because they change over time. What you found to be personally satisfying and productive at one point in your life, say 10 to 15 years ago, may be unproductive for you now or at a later stage. People "burn out" on jobs, or they become "dead wood."

Self-assessment is hard work. You have to want to do it, and you have to be able to cope with who you are. But this hard work has its rewards. Among the most important results are increased self-confidence and self-worth, as documented by your own achievements. These are the psychological tools you need to implement your marketing plan.

This chapter focuses on your personal opinions, values, attitudes, beliefs as they relate to career and employment. Completing these exercises can benefit your reemployment plans in a number of ways:

- They assist you in becoming a focused person so you can set clear future career goals.
- They provide you with an accurate set of words or phrases that you can use to describe yourself and your qualifications during a job interview.
- They help identify the kind of company, organization, or work group you are seeking. In a job interview, you can ask specific questions to determine how well the work environment suits your needs.
- They help establish criteria for evaluating job offers.
- You become more in touch with your current pattern of values, the ones that have and have not changed over the years. You are able to answer what is more important to you as you initiate a reemployment program.

The exercises in this chapter move from the general to the specific, that is, from general attitudes about your career to work-related values, valuing patterns, work motives, and preferred work environments. By completing the chapter, you are able to summarize what is important in your future employment. This information can help formulate your job search plans.*

EXERCISE 3–1: CAREER ATTITUDE ORIENTATION CONTINUUM

Purpose

From the social sciences, we know that attitudes or beliefs are basic orientations to the way we act or behave. It follows that career behavior flows from our attitudes about jobs and career. As you begin the assessment phase of your reemployment program, reflect on your personal convictions.

The Attitude Orientation Continuum exercise presents 16 attitudes or beliefs relating to you and your career. Each of the 8 items in the exercise is paired with its opposite. For example, in the first exercise, Action-Oriented is one extreme, and Reserved is the opposite. Of course, not everyone falls at either extreme. So the continuum is graded 9 through 1, with 9 representing one extreme and 1 the other. The numbers in between reflect the intervening spectrum. The numbers have no other specific meaning.

Instructions

Indicate your personal opinion about your career by circling the appropriate number on each continuum. In circling a number, you also indicate the way your personal beliefs effects your career behavior.

1. *Action-Oriented* _____ Reserved

9	8	7	6	5	4	3	2	1
Make career opportunities happen for me						Wait for others to cause career opportunities to happen to me		

2. *People-Oriented* _____ *Systems-Oriented*

9	8	7	6	5	4	3	2	1
Interact with individuals or groups						Interact with process systems, mechanical systems, or operations		

*Inspired by the Values Clarification strategies developed by colleagues and associates at Sagamore Institute, Saratoga Springs, N.Y.

3. Competition-Oriented   Cooperation-Oriented

9	8	7	6	5	4	3	2	1

Control my relationships   Involved in mutual
with others   developmental activities

4. Risk-Oriented   Security-Oriented

9	8	7	6	5	4	3	2	1

Personal choice have high   Personal choice that
probability for failure   minimize chances for
       failure

5. Task-Oriented   Relationship-Oriented

9	8	7	6	5	4	3	2	1

Concerned primarily with   Primarily concerned
accomplishing career goals   with maintaining personal
and activities   relationships as means
       of career success

6. Planning-Oriented   Intuition/Impulse-Orientation

9	8	7	6	5	4	3	2	1

Believes that future career   Take career actions
can be improved through active   quickly without a
intervention now with a detailed road map   developed plan

7. Open-Oriented   Private-Oriented

9	8	7	6	5	4	3	2	1

Believes in discussing career   Little need to openly
plans and goals with supervisors and peers   discuss career plans;
       keeps to oneself

8. Future-Oriented   Past-Oriented

9	8	7	6	5	4	3	2	1

Makes plans and takes actions   Concerned about past
to maximize career in the future   accomplishments or oversights

After completing this exercise, summarize what you have learned or relearned about yourself. Write a series of short statements based on your reactions to the exercise, explaining how your reactions may effect your future career goals.

Examples

I believe I am a very impulsive person because I have changed jobs a number of times without thinking through the long range consequences it had on my career. I plan on becoming more future-oriented in my career development.

As I look back, I realize that I am more concerned about what has *happened* to me in my dealings with bosses. I tend to be reactive to past situations. I would like to anticipate my reactions to superiors by being more prepared and to deal positively with situations.

I am an action-oriented, highly competitive, and aggressive salesperson who will risk a lot when I think I'm going to win. I'm talkative and impulsive, with a strong concern about my future and future sales.

Some strong beliefs and attitudes I have about my career are:

_____

_____

_____

_____

_____

_____

Come back to this statement in Chapter 5 and 9, when you are preparing your career objective and writing the first draft of your resume.

EXERCISE 3–2: ATTITUDES ABOUT WORK

Purpose

Each of us has a set of attitudes and values about our work. These values act as filters through which we view life, coloring our personal expectations about jobs and careers. Usually, we inherit our values from someone or from a group of people.

Possibly, your current values represent a rejection by some person or group. By analyzing where your values originated and how they may have changed over time, you can better understand your value perceptions about past or future jobs. Where do you think you got your values from? Your parents? Siblings? Colleagues? Supervisors? Mentors?

Instructions

In this exercise, eight general opinion statements or assumptions are listed in the left-hand column of Table 3–1. In the first column to the right of each statement, marked "Self," circle an **A** if you agree with the statement or a **D** if you disagree with it. Then do the same for the other columns, headed "Mother," "Father," and so on. If you think your mother agrees with the statement, circle the **A**; if you think she disagrees, circle the **D**. After you do so for each statement, add the number of **A**s and **D**s for each column and place the sums in "Totals." Then answer the Reflections Questions that follow.

Reflection questions

1. Which group is most similar to your response?

   _____

2. Which group(s) did you most agree with (highest number of As)?

   _____

3. Which group(s) did you most disagree with (highest number of Ds)?

   _____

4. Where do you think your values originated?

   _____

5. How have your values about work changed in the past ten years? Would you change the **A**s and **D**s if you could?

   _____

   _____

   _____

TABLE 3–1
ATTITUDES ABOUT WORK

	Self	Mother	Father	Siblings	Colleagues	Superiors and Supervisors	Mentors
1. Most people are basically lazy and don't like to work.	A D	A D	A D	A D	A D	A D	A D
2. If anyone works hard enough, he/she can be successful.	A D	A D	A D	A D	A D	A D	A D
3. In this world, it's each person for himself/herself.	A D	A D	A D	A D	A D	A D	A D
4. You can get ahead today only if you have a good education.	A D	A D	A D	A D	A D	A D	A D
5. Men make better managers than women.	A D	A D	A D	A D	A D	A D	A D
6. People move ahead only because they know people.	A D	A D	A D	A D	A D	A D	A D
7. The bottom line's the only thing that counts.	A D	A D	A D	A D	A D	A D	A D
8. Nice guys finish last.	A D	A D	A D	A D	A D	A D	A D
Totals	As ___ Ds ___	As ___ Ds ___	As ___ Ds ___	As ___ Ds ___	As ___ Ds ___	As ___ Ds ___	As ___ Ds ___

6. Which group(s) did you find most difficult to assess? Why do you think that happened?

_____

_____

_____

7. Which values would you most like to change in the next five years?

_____

_____

_____

8. What can you do now to begin that change?

● _____

● _____

● _____

EXERCISE 3–3: PERSONAL MOTIVATION FOR WORKING

Purpose

Raths, Harmin, and Simon define values as "those elements which show how a person has decided to use his/her life." Work values are those aspects of our work experience that we regard as important sources of satisfaction.

Many different values motivate people to work. Some values change in time, others don't. Numerous theories have been proposed and studies developed on work and motivation in the past eighty years, many of which point to the fact that values or motives are a key ingredient in a personal career development and satisfaction.

What are your work values? We are not espousing a new theory. The purpose of this exercise is to help you clarify your values and motives. At a very basic level, Why do you work?

Instructions

Study the list of 30 reasons why people work in Figure 3–3. The list is not exhaustive, but it contains many of the reasons that researchers have advanced over the years. You are to select the primary reasons that you work. Since choosing from a long list may be difficult, this exercise uses a process of elimination to arrive at your critical or most important values.

1. Circle the ten values that are most important to you at this time, and write them in the spaces provided.

_____   _____

_____   _____

_____   _____

_____   _____

_____   _____

FIGURE 3–3

THIRTY REASONS THAT PEOPLE WORK

1. Acquire material goods; have a comfortable and prosperous life
2. Advance in organization
3. Gain power to influence others
4. Assume responsibility
5. Get ahead/financial improvement
6. Variety of tasks; doing new and different tasks
7. To be directed by others
8. Accomplish personal goals.
9. Make a profit for company
10. Provide for exciting, active, and stimulating life
11. Stay off welfare
12. Attain economic security, assure dependable, stable income and benefits
13. Greater recognition and respect from others
14. More authority to direct others
15. Contribute to social needs of others; be of service to others
16. Make lots of money
17. Run own organization
18. Be a team member; enjoying congenial co-workers
19. Gain knowledge and skills to improve one's competency and knowledge
20. Freedom to direct self
21. Socio-economic status
22. Make a lasting contribution to society
23. Acceptance and sense of belonging with others
24. Dependence on others
25. Creativity and challenge
26. Identify new problems and produce new and original work
27. Moral value; behavior consistent with a moral code
28. Self-respect
29. Adventure; deal with situations that involve risks and change
30. Self-expression; behavior consistent with one's self-concept

2. From the list of ten, identify the top five values, and write them below.
3. Eliminate one of your top five, and write your top four values on the second line.
4. Eliminate one of your top four, and write your top three values on the third line.
5. Eliminate one of your top three, and write your top two values on the fourth line.
6. Eliminate one of your top two, and write your most important value on the bottom line.
7. Transfer this self-information to the Career Summary Sheets on page 91 in the Personal Values Section. The results of this exercise can be useful in a sales presentation or when you are preparing responses to interviewers' questions on page 192.

Top
Five _____ _____ _____ _____ _____

Top
Four   _____ _____ _____ _____

Top
Three   _____ _____ _____

Top
Two   _____ _____

Top
One   _____

EXERCISE 3–4:
EXPECTATION/SATISFACTION DIFFERENTIAL INDEX

The *satisfaction/dissatisfaction level* of your job or career is the degree of congruence between your key personal motives or values for working and the actual results you derive from working. It is the degree of correspondence between what you expect and what you get. If you judge the actual outcome of the value to be *better than* or *equal to* what you expect, you feel satisfied.

Actual Consequences $\geq$ Expected Consequences

If, on the other hand, you decide that the actual outcomes are *less than* what you expect, you probably are dissatisfied with your job/career.

Actual Consequences $\leq$ Expected Consequences

The attractiveness of your job/career is either enhanced or diminished by your current satisfaction level regarding the things you consider important. The Expectation/Satisfaction Differential Index is designed to measure the degree of congruence between what you want and what you get from your career.

Instructions

1. In Table 3–2, read through the work values and motives on the left.
2. The numbers to the right of each value or motive, in the columns marked "Expected" and "Actual," represent a range from "a great deal" (5) to "very little" (1). Circle the number appropriate to your situation.
3. Compute the Score Differential by adding both numbers and putting the sum in the third column.
4. Then following the instructions at the end of the table.

Example

	What I Expect From My Job					What My Last Job Actually Provided Me					Score Differential
	A great deal	A lot	Some	Little	Very little	A great deal	A lot	Some	Little	Very little	
Salary	(−5)	−4	−3	−2	−1	+5	+4	(+3)	+2	+1	−2
Power and Authority	−5	−4	(−3)	−2	−1	+5	(+4)	+3	+2	+1	+1
Personal Growth	−5	−4	−3	(−2)	−1	+5	+4	+3	(+2)	+1	0
Total Differential Score											−1

TABLE 3–2

EXPECTATION/SATISFACTION DIFFERENTIAL INDEX

	What I Expect From My Job					What My Last Job Actually Provided Me					Score Differential
	A great deal	*A lot*	*Some*	*Little*	*Very little*	*A great deal*	*A lot*	*Some*	*Little*	*Very little*	
1. Salary	−5	−4	−3	−2	−1	+5	+4	+3	+2	+1	_____
2. Employee benefits	−5	−4	−3	−2	−1	+5	+4	+3	+2	+1	_____
3. Economic security	−5	−4	−3	−2	−1	+5	+4	+3	+2	+1	_____
4. Recognition from bosses and peers	−5	−4	−3	−2	−1	+5	+4	+3	+2	+1	_____
5. Social status	−5	−4	−3	−2	−1	+5	+4	+3	+2	+1	_____
6. Future promotions and opportunities	−5	−4	−3	−2	−1	+5	+4	+3	+2	+1	_____
7. Challenging activities	−5	−4	−3	−2	−1	+5	+4	+3	+2	+1	_____
8. Meaningful work	−5	−4	−3	−2	−1	+5	+4	+3	+2	+1	_____
9. Increased power and authority	−5	−4	−3	−2	−1	+5	+4	+3	+2	+1	_____
10. Opportunity to learn new skills	−5	−4	−3	−2	−1	+5	+4	+3	+2	+1	_____
11. Personal growth and self-worth	−5	−4	−3	−2	−1	+5	+4	+3	+2	+1	_____
12. Sense of achievement	−5	−4	−3	−2	−1	+5	+4	+3	+2	+1	_____
13. Enhanced reputation in profession and community	−5	−4	−3	−2	−1	+5	+4	+3	+2	+1	_____
14. Responsibility over people	−5	−4	−3	−2	−1	+5	+4	+3	+2	+1	_____
15. Fast-paced, competitive environment	−5	−4	−3	−2	−1	+5	+4	+3	+2	+1	_____
16. Independence, directing my own behavior	−5	−4	−3	−2	−1	+5	+4	+3	+2	+1	_____
17. Friendly, congenial co-workers	−5	−4	−3	−2	−1	+5	+4	+3	+2	+1	_____

TABLE 3–2

(Cont.)

	What I Expect From My Job					What My Last Job Actually Provided Me					Score Differential
	A great deal	*A lot*	*Some*	*Little*	*Very little*	*A great deal*	*A lot*	*Some*	*Little*	*Very little*	
18. Short work hours/longer vacations	−5	−4	−3	−2	−1	+5	+4	+3	+2	+1	_____
19. Work-related social activities	−5	−4	−3	−2	−1	+5	+4	+3	+2	+1	_____
20. Self-respect and self-esteem	−5	−4	−3	−2	−1	+5	+4	+3	+2	+1	_____
21. Variety of tasks, doing new and different activities	−5	−4	−3	−2	−1	+5	+4	+3	+2	+1	_____
22. Exciting, stimulating life	−5	−4	−3	−2	−1	+5	+4	+3	+2	+1	_____
23. Creativity; producing new and original work	−5	−4	−3	−2	−1	+5	+4	+3	+2	+1	_____
24. Interpersonal relationships; sense of belonging to a group	−5	−4	−3	−2	−1	+5	+4	+3	+2	+1	_____
25. Dependence, work guided by others	−5	−4	−3	−2	−1	+5	+4	+3	+2	+1	_____
26. Self-expression	−5	−4	−3	−2	−1	+5	+4	+3	+2	+1	_____
27. Opportunity to travel	−5	−4	−3	−2	−1	+5	+4	+3	+2	+1	_____
28. Make high-risk decisions	−5	−4	−3	−2	−1	+5	+4	+3	+2	+1	_____
29. Prestige	−5	−4	−3	−2	−1	+5	+4	+3	+2	+1	_____
30, Other:	−5	−4	−3	−2	−1	+5	+4	+3	+2	+1	_____
31. _____	−5	−4	−3	−2	−1	+5	+4	+3	+2	+1	_____
32. _____	−5	−4	−3	−2	−1	+5	+4	+3	+2	+1	_____
33. _____	−5	−4	−3	−2	−1	+5	+4	+3	+2	+1	_____
34. _____	−5	−4	−3	−2	−1	+5	+4	+3	+2	+1	_____
35. _____	−5	−4	−3	−2	−1	+5	+4	+3	+2	+1	_____
Total Score Differential											

Scoring procedure

Add all the Score Differentials in the third column, and place the total in the appropriate blank. Your score can be positive, negative, or zero.

Scoring interpretation

If your Total Differential Score is between:

- +20 and +120   Your employment situation provides you with more than you expect. This could indicate high satisfaction. However, the problem that you have may be that you set low expectations of yourself or of your job situation.

- +20 and −20   More than likely you are satisfied with your job or career. Your level of congruence between what you want from your job and what it provides is satisfying to you at this time.

- −20 and −120   You are generally dissatisfied with your job and lack significant congruence between what you want from your job and what you receive. Your problem may be that you are setting unrealistic goals for yourself and finding it difficult to fulfill them. You may either have to change and lower your expectations, or find new, more realistic ways of fulfilling your goals and expectations.

Reflection questions

Go back and review the 30 value items in Table 3–2, and identify the 10 that are most important to you. List them below in their order of importance, with 1 being the most important.

1. _____   6. _____

2. _____   7. _____

3. _____   8. _____

4. _____   9. _____

5. _____   10. _____

Transfer these value items to the Personal Values section in the Career Summary on page 91. Then reflect on the following questions:

1. When you study the ten most important value items in your career, do you notice any specific pattern in terms of your expectations and results?

2. Did you find that most of the score differentials were zero, meaning that you got what you expected from your last job?

3. Did you discover that you desired more from your last job than you actually received? A pattern like −5 or −4 on the expectation side or +3 or +1 on the actual side indicates such an outcome.

4. Did you see a pattern of little expectations (−2 or −1) and high actual results (+5 or +4)?

5. Finally, did you discover any set pattern within your ten most important value items?

6. Do you find that your top ten expectations are met in your present (or most recent) job? If not, what can you do to have them met in your next job? Complete the following Can Do List by identifying some actions that incorporate your values:

Can Do List

- _____
- _____
- _____
- _____
- _____

EXERCISE 3–5: ANALYZING YOUR WORK ENVIRONMENT*

Purpose

Interviewers often question you about your motives, long-range career goals, and ideal work situations. A thorough assessment of your work climate may pay off during your marketing activities, when you may have to respond promptly to such interview questions as:

*Adapted from strategies designed by Jack Bologna.

- Describe your past work situations.
- What did you dislike about your past job?
- What kind of work environments do you function best in?
- What kind of conflicts have you had with past employers?
- What are your key career motives?

Management scientists have studied work climates or environments for decades due to the close relationship between personal job/career satisfaction, productivity, and performance. An assessment of various work environments is an indirect method of determining your personal motives. This exercise helps to clarify the kinds of work situations in which you are the most and least productive and consequently the most or least satisfied.

Instructions

How would you describe your recent and preferred work climate? The words in the following list describe various work situations. Study this list.

Growing	Orderly	Monotonous	Rigid
Paternal	Uncomfortable	Congenial	Uncontrolled
Complex	Productive	Controlled	Imaginative
Structured	Polite	Unfair	Cheerful
Educational	Profitable	Responsive	Ethical
Artistic	Restricted	Aggressive	Warm
Unresponsive	Harmonious	Helpful	Open
Depressing	Pleasant	Cooperative	Communicative
Unfriendly	Discouraging	Fast-moving	Exciting
Respectful	Youthful	Fulfilling	Peaceful
Dishonest	Moody	Compatible	Comfortable
Hectic	Argumentative	Rewarding	Challenging
Unrewarding	Old	Uncongenial	Happy
Lonely	Fair	Unexciting	Honest
Unpleasant	Political	Close-knit	Intellectual
Slow	Expanding	Uncooperative	Boring
Technical	Demanding	Impolite	
Cyclical	Friendly	Supportive	

Column 1

1. _____
2. _____
3. _____
4. _____
5. _____
6. _____
7. _____

Column 2

1. _____
2. _____
3. _____
4. _____
5. _____
6. _____
7. _____

Column 3

1. _____
2. _____
3. _____
4. _____
5. _____
6. _____
7. _____

Column 4

1. _____
2. _____
3. _____
4. _____
5. _____
6. _____
7. _____

Reflection questions

1. What kind of gap exists between your Columns 1 and 3?

_____

_____

_____

_____

_____

2. What can you do to change or narrow the gap?

_____

_____

_____

_____

_____

Analysis of columns

This exercise can be helpful when you're preparing your responses to the most asked interview questions on page 191. Particularly, the information from Column 3 is helpful in describing your responses to questions about your preferred work environment.

When you look at the way you described your most recent work environment in Column 1, do you find that these words are colored by your emotional reaction to involuntary termination? Would you have said the same thing about your job six months ago? Do you have negative feelings about your past boss or employer?

Experiencing a negative reaction to being terminated is perfectly normal. During an interview, however, there is a major difference between feeling hostile or angry and speaking negatively about your past supervisor or employer. Never speak negatively about anyone during an interview. If you are negative now, what could you have said about your employer six months or a year ago?

EXERCISE 3–6: SUMMARY OF VALUES AND MOTIVES

Write out a brief statement explaining the conclusions you drew from working through this chapter.

1. My expectations/satisfaction level about my job:

   _____

   _____

   _____

   _____

   _____

2. My work environment:

   _____

   _____

   _____

   _____

   _____

3. As a result of these insights, I resolve:

_____

_____

_____

_____

_____

Transcribe significant data from this section to the Career Analysis Summary.

References for Further Reading

Goodman, Joel, ed. *Turning Points, New Developments, New Directions in Values Clarification*. Saratoga Springs, N.Y.: Creative Resources Press, 1978.

Raths, Louis, Merrill Harmin, and Sidney B. Simon. *Values and Teaching*. Columbus, Ohio: Merrill Publishing Company, 1966.

Simon, Sidney B., Howard Kirschenbaum, and Leland Howe. *Values Clarification*. New York: Hart, 1972.

Stoner, James A. F., *et al. Managerial Career Plateaus*. New York: Columbia University, Graduate School of Business, 1980.

Storey, Walter D. *Career Dimensions, I & II*. New York: General Electric, Inc., Croton-on-Hudson, N.Y., 1976.

4

Assessment of career skills

A job is composed of a series of related tasks or activities. Skills or competencies represent the abilities of each person to accomplish these tasks. Skill identification is therefore a critical aspect of the reemployment process. What are skills? Generally, they are actions—things that you *do*. They can represent your strengths, your key abilities, specific knowledges you have, characteristics that give you potential, the ways you tend to be most successful when dealing with problems, tasks, or life experiences. Essentially, they reveal what makes you a unique person.

Figure 4–1 presents the tasks and related skills of a sales manager. Two tasks of a sales manager, for example, are selling and managing staff. In Figure 4–1, we can assume that for Task 1, selling, sales managers need to use the skills of Developing trust and rapport with the prospects or customers (Skill 1). They must use their influencing ability (Skill 2), as well as their ability to arbitrate or negotiate terms of sale (Skill 3). Task 2, managing a sales staff, requires a number of skills, one of which is arbitrating differences between staff members—the same skill as Skill 3 in Task 1. However, managing also involves problem solving (Skill 4) and evaluation of individual performance (Skill 5).

In the reemployment process, it is important to use words or phrases that describe your skills:

- I develop rapport and trust with people very quickly.
- I speak clearly and effectively.
- I can motivate people.

The interviewer makes decisions about possible job-person matches while listening to your sales presentation about your qualifications and abilities. However, this task of skill identification is difficult because most people have a limited set of words they use to describe themselves. This chapter helps you to develop a set of words, so that you can thoroughly describe your abilities and talents to the interviewer. If an interviewer were to ask you the following questions, how strong would your sales presentation be?

- Tell me about yourself.
- What are your three most significant accomplishments?
- How do you think we would be able to most effectively use you here at _____?
- What are your greatest competencies?
- In looking back, which job did you most like and why?
- Which one did you most dislike and why?

To be able to answer these questions, you need self-information about your skills. Exercise 4–1 is based on an effective skill-identifying method that yields this information.

FIGURE 4–1

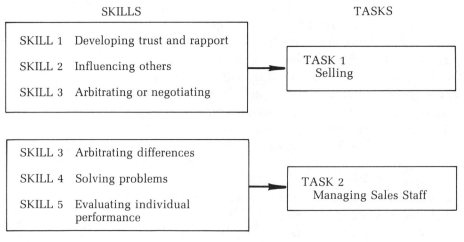

SKILLS   TASKS

SKILL 1   Developing trust and rapport

SKILL 2   Influencing others   TASK 1
                                              Selling
SKILL 3   Arbitrating or negotiating

SKILL 3   Arbitrating differences

SKILL 4   Solving problems   TASK 2
                                              Managing Sales Staff
SKILL 5   Evaluating individual
          performance

The method is a modification of Bernard Haldane's System to Identify Motivated Skills (SIMS) in his book *Career Satisfaction and Success: A Guide to Job Freedom*, and of Richard Bolles' autobiographical approach to skill identification in *What Color Is Your Parachute?*

EXERCISE 4–1: CAREER RENEWAL PLAN

Instructions

To begin your Career Renewal Plan, write out ten to fifteen events or situations from your life experience that have great significance and meaning for you.

In the first paragraph of the Accomplishment section, describe each event in terms of some personal achievement, peak experience, key event, period of time, job, work situation, or project that you feel positive about and enjoyed doing. Do not limit your thinking to work situations. Include situations from family life, community, social or religious activities, avocation or hobbies, and other areas. In each situation, stress what you did, how you did it, with whom, at what odds, with what resources, and for what rewards.

In the second paragraph of the Value section, describe how each event affected you. What was it about the event that was so important to you? What was it that you seek, feel, believe, hold important, or want to experience that this accomplishment provided? Record your Value Reasons in this section.

Write each section in paragraph form, using as many additional sheets of paper as necessary.

Accomplishment

_____

_____

_____

_____

_____

_____

Value

_____

_____

_____

_____

_____

_____

_____

_____

_____

_____

_____

_____

_____

_____

_____

_____

EXERCISE 4–2: THE SKILLS/VALUES IDENTIFICATION PROCESS

The Skills/Values Identification Process demands a significant amount of your time and energy. It may even help you to have your spouse/close friend work through this process with you. However you complete it, do not cheat yourself by skimming these pages. Expending the effort now will pay off in the future when writing your resume and sitting in job interviews. You will be able to concisely state your skills and document them with examples for a strong, persuasive marketing presentation.

Instructions

1. Review your ten to fifteen events or situations from Exercise 4–1. Number them according to any criterion that you choose. Number 1 should be the most valued. Your criteria for ranking them may be: the one you most *enjoyed* achieving, the one you're most *proud* of, or the one that has the greatest *value* to you.

2. After you have completed your ranking, read your first achievement aloud. With a red pen in hand, look for and underscore the "action" verbs and phrases to make them stand out. You might ask yourself the "what," "who," "where," "when," and "how" questions. You may also find the following list of "skill words" helpful in this identification process:

Achieving	Completing	Devising	Filing
Advancing	Composing	Directing	Figuring
Advising	Conceiving	Documenting	Forecasting
Analyzing	Conducting	Editing	Formulating
Applying	Controlling	Effecting	Founding
Arranging	Coordinating	Eliminating	Forming
Assembling	Counseling	Enforcing	Generating
Assessing	Creating	Establishing	Guiding
Auditing	Decreasing	Evaluating	Heading
Bargaining	Demonstrating	Executing	Hiring
Building	Designing	Expanding	Illustrating
Collaborating	Determining	Expediting	Implementing
Communicating	Developing	Facilitating	Improving

Initiating	Measuring	Providing	Speaking
Inspecting	Motivating	Publishing	Staffing
Inspiring	Negotiating	Recommending	Starting
Instructing	Navigating	Reconciling	Studying
Installing	Operating	Recruiting	Supervising
Interviewing	Organizing	Reducing	Surveying
Investigating	Originating	Reporting	Terminating
Joining	Performing	Researching	Testing
Leading	Persuading	Resolving	Training
Learning	Piloting	Restoring	Translating
Launching	Planning	Revising	Uniting
Listening	Preparing	Saving	Utilizing
Making	Presenting	Scheduling	Winning
Maintaining	Processing	Selecting	Writing
Managing	Producing	Singing	
Marketing	Promoting	Solving	

3. After you underscore the key action verbs and phrases, begin listing these skills in the upper left-hand corner of the Skill Identification Worksheet (Figure 4–3).

4. After completing the Skills column, reread the achievement for the purpose of identifying your values. Seek out the reasons that this achievement is important to you. List the words you have used or interpretations you now see in this achievement In the Values column of the Skill Identification Worksheet (Figure 4–3).

5. After you have thoroughly analyzed the first situation, move on to the next achievement, and identify the skills and values that it reveals.

6. Continue until you have analyzed all your achievements.

7. Don't be surprised if you find yourself repeating the same skill and value words. Write the words on the list each time you think they apply. This is not a time for false modesty. The more often the same words appear, the stronger your pattern of skills/values.

This process is illustrated in Figure 4–2.

FIGURE 4–2

Achievement	Skills	Values
1. Going Away to College It was significant for many reasons. It was an *opportunity for independence*. I was *confronting* all the *decisions* of living on *my own*. The experience of living with other women was *challenging* since my background had been primarily with men. The *friendships I formed* have impacted my life. *I struggled* with calculus my first year (math being my intended major) to the point that I *changed* my major. *Choosing economics* was another *challenge* as I was the *only one* in my class majoring in this area. My classes were small, tending toward *independent studies*. It was also a *financial struggle* to *support myself working* my way through a private college. *My organizational skills* were first employed with *recognized success* in the admissions office. My college experience was *challenging* but *maturing*.	1. Communications 2. Human Relations 3. Decision making (choosing) 4. Organization 5. Planning 6. Setting goals 7. Verbal Communication/speaking 8. Leadership 9. Adapting/flexible 10. Coping 11. Problem solving 12. Managing time 13. Coping with pressure	1. Independence 2. Challenge 3. Recognized success 4. Freedom/liberating 5. Personal choice 6. Friendships 7. New Opportunities 8. Self-motivating
2. My *decision to enter a graduate program* came several years after getting my BA. The *hesitancy* was probably the result of the different experiences I had in obtaining a job after my first degree. *I was beginning a program* when my friends had completed their masters. *I selected* a masters in *management* that was more general, but academically *challenging*. It was personally *rewarding to meet and work* closely with people from other occupations and backgrounds. My *current job frustration comes from not using the knowledge or skills I obtained from this program*.	1. Decision making 2. Set goals 3. Learning/studying the skills 4. Evaluating alternatives 5. Time management 6. Planning 7. Organizing 8. Follow-through 9. Research 10. Analyzing 11. Communication	1. Motivation 2. Challenge 3. Choosing 4. Self-direction 5. Independence 6. Personal Security

FIGURE 4–3
SKILL IDENTIFICATION WORKSHEET

Event No. ____ (Priority)
Skills: Values:

Event No. ____ (Priority)
Skills: Values:

Event No. ____ *(Priority)*
Skills: *Values:*

Event No. ____ *(Priority)*
Skills: *Values:*

FIGURE 4–3
(Cont.)

Event No. —— (Priority)
Skills:

_____

_____

_____

_____

_____

_____

Values:

_____

_____

_____

_____

_____

_____

Event No. —— (Priority)
Skills:

_____

_____

_____

_____

_____

_____

Values:

_____

_____

_____

_____

_____

_____

Event No. —— (Priority)
Skills:

_____

_____

_____

_____

_____

_____

Values:

_____

_____

_____

_____

_____

_____

Event No. —— (Priority)
Skills:

_____

_____

_____

_____

_____

_____

Values:

_____

_____

_____

_____

_____

_____

EXERCISE 4–3: MASTER LIST OF SKILLS

Instructions

After completing the Skills/Values Identification, develop your Master List of Skills. To do so, simply transcribe the information from the Skill Identification Worksheet. Begin by copying the skills from your first achievement, and then add to the list any new skill words from the second achievement. Based on the example in Figure 4–2, the beginning of the "Master Skills List" would look like this:

1. Communications	10. Coping
2. Human relations	11. Problem solving
3. Decision making	12. Managing time
4. Organizing	13. Coping with pressure
5. Planning	14. Learning/studying
6. Setting goals	15. Evaluating
7. Speaking	16. Follow-through
8. Leadership	17. Research
9. Adapting/flexible	18. Analyzing

List a word only once. Then go back and count how many times each skill word is actually used.

	Skill	How Often Used		Skill	How Often Used
1.	_____	____	10.	_____	____
2.	_____	____	11.	_____	____
3.	_____	____	12.	_____	____
4.	_____	____	13.	_____	____
5.	_____	____	14.	_____	____
6.	_____	____	15.	_____	____
7.	_____	____	16.	_____	____
8.	_____	____	17.	_____	____
9.	_____	____	18.	_____	____

	Skill	*How Often Used*		Skill	*How Often Used*
19.	_____	____	32.	_____	____
20.	_____	____	33.	_____	____
21.	_____	____	34.	_____	____
22.	_____	____	35.	_____	____
23.	_____	____	36.	_____	____
24.	_____	____	37.	_____	____
25.	_____	____	38.	_____	____
26.	_____	____	39.	_____	____
27.	_____	____	40.	_____	____
28.	_____	____	41.	_____	____
29.	_____	____	42.	_____	____
30.	_____	____	43.	_____	____
31.	_____	____	44.	_____	____

From your Master List of Skills, select six to ten major skills or groups of skills that you want to use in your next job. They may well be the skills that you have used most often in the past. Therefore, thoroughly scrutinize the skills that appeared at least five times on your Master List. List these skills below:

1.	_____	6.	_____	
2.	_____	7.	_____	
3.	_____	8.	_____	
4.	_____	9.	_____	
5.	_____	10.	_____	

Study this refined list. Are these your Motivated Skills? That is, are they the ones that you do competently as well as *enjoy*? Eliminate any that may be Unmotivated Skills—those that you do well but don't enjoy. Now prioritize this list so that the foremost skill from the preceding list represents the skill or competency that you *most* want to use in your next job. The second is the next most important, and so on.

1. _____   5. _____

2. _____   6. _____

3. _____   7. _____

4. _____   8. _____

Transcribe this list to your Career Analysis Summary on page 92.

This skill analysis prepares you for writing your resume in two ways:

1. The important skills areas or groups can be used in the development of your objective statement on pages 83, 154.
2. Documentation or "proofs" of these skills can be used in writing your Achievement section on page 156. The proof of each skill should consist of specific examples from your past experience that demonstrate your skill competence. Write out these examples in 25 words or less, starting with strong action verbs (see the list in Exercise 4–2).

EXERCISE 4–4: CAREER PROGRESSION ASSESSMENT TOOL

Purpose

As defined in Robert Oliver's book, *Career Unrest: A Source of Creativity*, career satisfaction is a process of your interaction with work itself within a particular work environment over a period of time. Each aspect is a part of a connected, three-part system, as illustrated in Figure 4–4.

Now that a period in your career history has ended and you prepare for your next career move, reviewing your career history is appropriate. You will be looking for patterns or trends that you have developed over time. You can also assess the stages of your career development to effectively plan your short-term and long-range goals.

The Career Progression Assessment Tool is a method of reviewing your professional career. Once it is completed, you

FIGURE 4–4

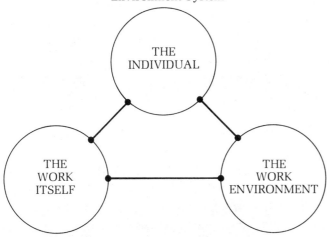

The Individual = Work = Work
Environment System

Reprinted with permission, Robert Oliver, *Career Unrest: A Source of Creativity* (New York: Columbia University), pp. 52 & 55.

see your periods of development and patterns of success. The selected data can then be used in the Professional Experience section of your resume. Please read the following instructions carefully before completing the worksheet. (See Figure 4–5).

Instructions

1. Start with your *present* or *most recent* position in the extreme left column and work backwards in your career history as you move across to the right-hand side of the worksheet.

2. Put your current age on the extreme left side of your first vertical column.

3. Specify your job title and function for each job that you have had. If you had a number of different positions with the same organization, fill in a vertical column for each position, treating each position as a separate job, including your age at the time the position/title was held.

4. Indicate the years of service for each job function.

5. Now work through each vertical column entirely before moving on to the next position.

6. List your major duties and responsibilities for this position. What was expected of you?

7. What do you think you contributed to your organization at this time? How is that firm better because of you? Don't feel that you had to receive any formal recognition to list your personal contributions here.
8. What aspects did you most *like* about the job or position?
9. What did you most *dislike* about your situation?
10. How would you describe your relationship with your boss? What words would your boss use to describe you in that position?
11. What status symbols did your organization associate with your position?
12. What type of progression did this position represent for your career? A promotion, a lateral transfer, a demotion?
13. Who was most responsible for this environment in your career? You, your boss, your spouse, the company?
14. What personal feelings did you experience as a result of the movement?
15. Indicate salary level and employee benefits.
16. Go back to item 6, and repeat the process for your next position.
17. If you have had more than six positions, use additional 8½″ × 11″ sheets.

FIGURE 4–5

ILLUSTRATION OF CAREER PROGRESSION ASSESSMENT TOOL

Age	*31*
Job Title/Function	*Academic Administrator and Research Assistant*
Years of Service	7
Major Responsibilities	Manager and Administrator Research and computer work Instructional support Budget planning Hired and trained support staff Project Planning

FIGURE 4–5
(Cont.)

Personal Contributions to Organization	Set up Testing Services section Revamped testing procedures Developed department's philosophy
What I Like Most About the Position	Contact with people Personal independence Research work
What I Dislike Most About the Position	Bureaucracy of large university Noncompletion of results Solving the same old problems over and over Inability to promote good people Ineffective, impulsive boss Too depended on by everyone
Relationship with Manager/Supervisor	Get along well with boss because I am an organizer and planner, results-oriented. A doer and he isn't. Complement his limitations.
Organizational Status Symbols Associated with Position	My own office Five buttons on my phone!
Type of Career Progression	Advancement and promotion
Person Most Responsible for Career Progression	Myself
Personal Feelings About Position	Enjoyed them and happy with the job at the time, but I have moved on now
Salary Level and Benefits	Mid-twenties; good benefits

FIGURE 4–6

CAREER PROGRESSION ANALYSIS TIME (IN YEARS)

Age			
Job Title/function			
Years of Service			
Major Responsibilities			
Personal Contributions to Organization			
What I Liked Most About the Position			
What I Disliked Most About the Position			
Relationship with Manager/Supervisor			
Organizational Status Symbols Associated with Position			
Type of Career Progression			
Person Most Responsible For Career Progression			
Personal Feelings About Position			
Salary Level and Benefits			

Interpretations

1. The analysis of my career history shows that I have

   _____

   _____

   _____

   _____

2. The major value trends I have acted upon are

   _____

   _____

   _____

   _____

3. In the future I resolve to

   _____

   _____

   _____

   _____

4. In the future I resolve *not* to

   _____

   _____

   _____

   _____

The information in the Career Progression Analysis can be used in a number of ways.

1. The information from the categories Job Title/Function, Years of Service, Major Responsibilities, Personal Contributions to Organization, and What I Liked Most about the Position can be used to write the entries in the first draft of the Work History section of your resume on page 157.

2. The discernment of employment patterns is helpful in future planning. First identify the major patterns that emerge, and place them in the "Employment Pattern"

section on your Career Summary Analysis page. This information can also be useful in preparing responses to such interviewer's questions as:

- Tell me about yourself.
- Briefly describe the stages of your career development to date.
- How would you assess your previous positions in terms of likes and dislikes?
- How would you describe your relationship with previous supervisors or managers?

3. This information can be used in setting personal goals. Behavioral scientists know that most people do not change their behavior patterns unless they consciously choose to—even then they resist changing. The career patterns do not radically change because you begin a new position in another organization. If a lack of planning got you into trouble with the past employer, it will do so again—unless you do something about it. If you have a history of problems with supervisors, more than likely it will continue. If the reason for your termination had to do with behavior problems, now is the time to plan a change in your action.

What trends do you wish to change in the future? What trends do you want to keep the same?

_____

_____

_____

_____

_____

_____

_____

_____

_____

EXERCISE 4–5: CAREER/LIFE SATISFACTION AT VARIOUS AGES

Researchers have distinguished between career unrest and life dissatisfaction. Both may take place at the same time and they may nurture each other, but they are two separate issues. *Career satisfaction* is usually related to our reactions about work and the work environment. *Life satisfaction* comes from family situations or from the communities we live in.

Instructions

The Career/Life Satisfaction Graph is a method of plotting degrees of satisfaction over periods of time in your life and career. Study the information you wrote in the Career Progression Analysis on page 60 before completing this graph. As shown in Figure 4–7a, the degrees of satisfaction from the vertical axis, while five-year age periods form the horizontal axis. Write your current age underneath the first vertical line on the left side of the graph. As you move to the right side of the graph, write your age in five-year segments until high school graduation.

To graph the long-term patterns, take a felt tip pen and draw a solid line on the Career/Life Satisfaction Graph. The solid line indicates the degree of satisfaction in your career. Take a felt tip pen of a different color and draw a broken line to indicate your degree of life satisfaction. Figure 4–7b shows a 55-year-old person with various levels of satisfaction and dissatisfaction. Upon completing the graphs, answer the following questions.

1. What's your reaction to your Career/Life Satisfaction Graph?

   _____

   _____

   _____

2. What can you do about it now?

   _____

   _____

   _____

FIGURE 4–7a

Career/Life satisfaction graph

DEGREE OF SATISFACTION

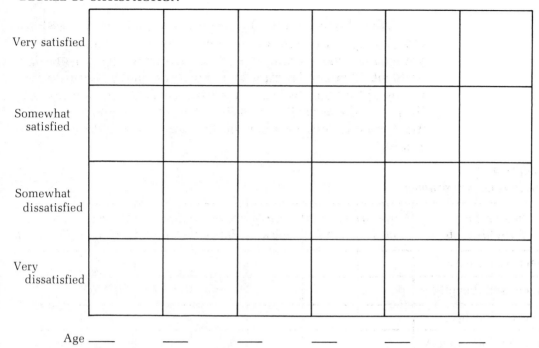

Age ___   ___   ___   ___   ___   ___

FIGURE 4–7b

DEGREE OF SATISFACTION

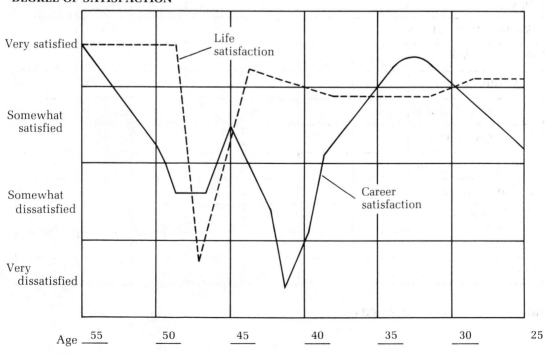

Age ___ 55 ___ 50 ___ 45 ___ 40 ___ 35 ___ 30 ___ 25

EXERCISE 4-6: HOW DID YOU GET TO BE WHERE YOU ARE TODAY?

Why did you move from job assignment to job assignment? Why did you make the moves you did? When assessing your career values and attitudes, reviewing the reasons for your job changes is important. For each move, indicate the reason(s) for your decision by putting an **X** on the appropriate fill-in or fill-ins in Figure 4-8. Let Job 1 correspond to your most recent job, as charted in your Career Progression Analysis.

FIGURE 4-8

CAREER VALUES AND ATTITUDES

Reason for Switching Job	Move to Job 1	Move to Job 2	Move to Job 3	Move to Job 4	Move to Job 5	Move to Job 6	Move to Job 7
Increased salary							
Increased benefits							
Greater prestige							
Broader job exposure							
Better location							
Health							
Graduate from school							
Was promoted							
Left military service							
Spouse was relocated							
Better organization							
Dissatisfied with job							
Lacked competence							
Unable to get along with boss							
To utilize skills							
Other:							

In looking back on your career history, how would you evaluate each decision now? Check off your responses in Figure 4–9.

FIGURE 4–9

EVALUATING YOUR JOB MOVES

	Move to Job 1	Move to Job 2	Move to Job 3	Move to Job 4	Move to Job 5	Move to Job 6	Move to Job 7
Excellent Move							
Good Move							
Uncertain							
Poor Move							

References for Further Reading

Bolles, Richard N. *What Color is Your Parachute?* (rev. ed.) Berkeley, Cal.: Ten Speed Press, 1980.

Figler, Howard. *The Complete Job-Search Handbook.* New York: Holt, Rinehart, & Winston, 1979.

Haldane, Bernard. *Career Satisfaction and Success: A Guide to Job Freedom.* New York: AMACOM, 1974.

Hagberg, Janet and Richard Leider. *The Inventurers.* Reading, Mass.: Addison, Wesley Publishing Company, 1979.

Oliver, Robert. *Career Unrest: A Source for Creativity.* New York: Columbia University, Graduate School of Business, 1981.

Stoner, James A.F., *et al. Managerial Career Plateaus: An Exploratory Study.* New York: Columbia University, Graduate School Of Business, 1980.

Storey, Walter D. *Career Dimensions II.* Croton-on-Hudson, N.Y.: General Electric Inc., 1976.

5

Life work planning: what are my options?

"Would you tell me please, which way I ought to walk from here?"

"That depends a good deal on where you want to get to." Alice in Wonderland

When people find themselves without jobs, they often develop tunnel vision regarding themselves and their future. Sometimes they think that they can do only the same job in the future as they did in the past. Or they think that their work has to be in the same industry or in the same geographic area. One of the major responsibilities of career counselors, however, is to help people develop options for themselves and to broaden their vision. You are limited only by the parameters that you set for yourself. At this point in your career, you have a number of alternatives to consider. They may include career change, relocation, early retirement, job search, and, for couples, dual-career lifestyle. These options can be represented as a decision fork, as shown in Figure 5–1.

Each option has a set of consequences for you, and you should thoroughly explore it in the process of making a decision about your future career and life. The next five chapters explore the consequences of each of these five options. We do not assume that all five are options for everyone. For example, if you have chosen a single lifestyle, the chapter on dual-career couples may not be extremely important. If you are in

OPTION		CONSEQUENCES

FIGURE 5-1:
OPTIONS AND CONSEQUENCES

your twenties or thirties, early retirement may be out of the question. While each of the next chapters has varying importance for you, we suggest that you read and work through as many options as possible. In this way, your decisions regarding life and career change will be thoroughly and rationally explored, and your commitment to these decisions can be definitive and satisfying.

Before beginning the exercises for this chapter, be aware of a common tendency of many individuals. These people live a "postponement" lifestyle.

- They wait till they find the right job, spouse, house—then they will . . .
- They wait till they become manager, partner, president—then they will . . .
- They wait till they have enough money—then they will . . .
- They wait till they retire—then they will . . .

You have only 168 hours to live each week. For a 35-year-old who expects to live until 75, that weekly figure totals up to 349,440 hours, with a normal breakdown like this:

	Per Day	In a Lifetime	Percentage
Sleep	8	116,480	33%
Work (includes commuting)	12	174,720	50%
Life Maintenance (eating, dressing, showering, and the like)	2.6	30,000	11%
Leisure time	1.4	28,240	6%
	24	349,440	100%

How many hours do you have to live? What are you planning to do with your scarce resource of time? To avoid the postponement lifestyle, you must assume an "active" role in planning your career/life future.

Planning is best described as *anticipatory decision making*. The planning tools in this chapter enable you to anticipate your future and to know the available alternatives. You will develop tentative career goals by examining your preference for the type of organization or industry, the preference for job function or title, the organizational level you can realistically work at, and geographically where you want to seek your next job. Addressing each of these four areas further defines, or puts more specific parameters around, "your job market."

EXERCISE 5–1: DEVELOPMENT OF TENTATIVE CAREER GOALS

Identify the type of industry or organization that you would prefer to work for in your next job. Rank order the top five by placing numbers in the blanks, 1 being most important, #2 second most important, and so on. After doing this for your next job, go on and do it for five years from now and ten years from now.

Next Job	5 Years	10 Years	
_____	_____	_____	Banking and finance
_____	_____	_____	Insurance
_____	_____	_____	Retail/wholesale
_____	_____	_____	Transportation
_____	_____	_____	Utilities
_____	_____	_____	Manufacturing
_____	_____	_____	Professional
_____	_____	_____	Education
_____	_____	_____	Hospital/health care
_____	_____	_____	Leisure/hotel/real estate
_____	_____	_____	Government
_____	_____	_____	Media

Next Job	5 Years	10 Years	Occupation
_____	_____	_____	Research and development
_____	_____	_____	Consulting
_____	_____	_____	Computer—high technology
_____	_____	_____	Other: _____

EXERCISE 5–2:
DEVELOPMENT OF TENTATIVE OCCUPATIONAL GOALS

People who are interested in changing careers should concentrate on this section. Often they find it difficult to identify job functions that they may wish to explore for short- or long-term careers.

Two major government publications, the *Dictionary of Occupational Titles* (DOT) and the *Occupational Outlook Handbook*, can be very helpful in providing detailed information on jobs. Both these volumes are readily available in local libraries, schools, community colleges, and other reference sources.

The *DOT* provides a broad perspective on interrelationships of occupations and career ladders. The *DOT* lists over 20,000 job titles. However, new jobs and new job titles are continually being created by technical change and by other factors affecting the labor/economic force. Also, as a result of technological, economic, and sociological influences nearly every job in the economy is performed slightly differently from any other job. Every job is also similar to a number of other jobs.

There are three different arrangements of occupational titles in the *DOT*: the Occupational Group arrangement, the Alphabetical Index, and Industry arrangement. The Occupational Group helps to identify closely related occupations, whereas the Industrial Group assists in identifying other jobs in an industry.

The Occupational Outlook Handbook offers detailed information on about 250 jobs. It covers the nature of the work, working conditions, employment training and other qualifications, advancement and job outlook earnings, related occupations, and sources of additional information.

Listed in this part of the goal-setting exercise is a very select list of jobs from the *DOT*.

- Professional, Technical, and Managerial Occupations
- Clerical occupations
- Sales occupations
- Service occupations
- Processing occupations
- Machine trade occupations

- Benchwork occupations
- Structural work occupations
- Transportation occupations
- Miscellaneous occupations
- Emerging occupations

Instructions

Read through the lists of selected occupations. If an occupation interests you for your next position, put a check next to it in the first column marked "Next Job." If you think it may be something you want to do in three to five years from now, put a check in the second column marked "5 years." If you think you may want to be functioning in that occupation seven to ten years from now, put a check in the third column marked "10 Years." After you have read through all the lists of the ten occupational groups, go back and prioritize the ones you have checked. Identify at least the top five occupations that you are most interested in for your next job, five years from now, and ten years from now. If you choose a position requiring additional education, you may have to allow a number of years for training as you project your future career plan. Now may well be the time to start your career in another direction.

PROFESSIONAL, TECHNICAL, MANAGERIAL

Next Job	5 Years	10 Years	Occupation
_____	_____	_____	Architect
_____	_____	_____	Engineer
_____	_____	_____	Electronics Technician
_____	_____	_____	Draftsman
_____	_____	_____	Systems Analyst

Next Job	5 Years	10 Years	Occupation
_____	_____	_____	Computer Programmer
_____	_____	_____	Chemist
_____	_____	_____	Forester
_____	_____	_____	Biologist
_____	_____	_____	Physicist
_____	_____	_____	Counselor
_____	_____	_____	Consultant
_____	_____	_____	Sociologist
_____	_____	_____	Psychologist
_____	_____	_____	Dentist
_____	_____	_____	Medical doctor
_____	_____	_____	Dentist
_____	_____	_____	Veterinarian
_____	_____	_____	Pharmacist
_____	_____	_____	Nurse
_____	_____	_____	Therapist
_____	_____	_____	Teacher
_____	_____	_____	Librarian
_____	_____	_____	Lawyer
_____	_____	_____	Auditor
_____	_____	_____	Accountant
_____	_____	_____	Estimator
_____	_____	_____	Purchasing agent
_____	_____	_____	Public relations
_____	_____	_____	Job analyst
_____	_____	_____	Inspector
_____	_____	_____	Underwriter
_____	_____	_____	Manager, industry

Next Job	5 Years	10 Years	Occupation
——	——	——	Funeral director
——	——	——	Supervisor, industry
——	——	——	Security officer
——	——	——	Social worker
——	——	——	Credit analysis
——	——	——	Air traffic controller
——	——	——	Financial analyst
——	——	——	Personnel officer
——	——	——	Researcher
——	——	——	Trainer
——	——	——	Mathematician
——	——	——	Scientist
——	——	——	Laboratory tester
——	——	——	Lab Technician
——	——	——	Dietician
——	——	——	Occupational therapist
——	——	——	Physical therapist
——	——	——	Dental hygienist
——	——	——	Medical technologist
——	——	——	Medical lab technician
——	——	——	Respiratory therapist
——	——	——	Medical assistant
——	——	——	Dental assistant
——	——	——	Administrative assistant
——	——	——	Manager, service industry
——	——	——	Manager, office
——	——	——	Manager, sales
——	——	——	Other: _____

CLERICAL

Next Job	5 Years	10 Years	Occupation
_____	_____	_____	Secretary
_____	_____	_____	Typist/word processor
_____	_____	_____	Clerk
_____	_____	_____	Bookkeeper
_____	_____	_____	Cashier
_____	_____	_____	Teller
_____	_____	_____	Receptionist
_____	_____	_____	Ticket agent
_____	_____	_____	Legal secretary
_____	_____	_____	Medical secretary
_____	_____	_____	Executive secretary

SALES

Next Job	5 Years	10 Years	Occupation
_____	_____	_____	Sales agent
_____	_____	_____	Manufacturer's marketing representative
_____	_____	_____	Account executive
_____	_____	_____	Sales manager
_____	_____	_____	Other: _____
_____	_____	_____	_____
_____	_____	_____	_____
_____	_____	_____	_____

SERVICE

Next Job	5 Years	10 Years	Occupation
_____	_____	_____	Waiter/waitress/bartender
_____	_____	_____	Chef/cook/baker
_____	_____	_____	Butcher/meat cutter
_____	_____	_____	Food services supervisor
_____	_____	_____	Barber/cosmetologist
_____	_____	_____	Flight attendant
_____	_____	_____	Nurse
_____	_____	_____	Fire fighter/police officer
_____	_____	_____	Janitor/maintenance
_____	_____	_____	Landscape gardener

TRANSPORTATION

Next Job	5 Years	10 Years	Occupation
_____	_____	_____	Tank truck driver
_____	_____	_____	Tractor trailer driver
_____	_____	_____	Transportation agent
_____	_____	_____	Bus/taxi driver
_____	_____	_____	Heavy equipment driver/operator
_____	_____	_____	Lubrication servicer
_____	_____	_____	Hi-lo driver
_____	_____	_____	Other: _____
_____	_____	_____	_____
_____	_____	_____	_____

PROCESSING

Next Job	5 Years	10 Years	Occupation
_____	_____	_____	Refinery operator
_____	_____	_____	Water treatment plant operator
_____	_____	_____	Machine operator
_____	_____	_____	Extruder operator
_____	_____	_____	Chemical operator
_____	_____	_____	Pilot control operator
_____	_____	_____	Laborer
_____	_____	_____	Other: _____

BENCH WORK

Next Job	5 Years	10 Years	Occupation
_____	_____	_____	Instrument mechanic
_____	_____	_____	Dental lab technician
_____	_____	_____	Watch repairer
_____	_____	_____	Radio repairer
_____	_____	_____	Electric motor repairer/assembler
_____	_____	_____	Electronics inspector/assembler
_____	_____	_____	Tire builder
_____	_____	_____	Cabinet assembler
_____	_____	_____	Furniture upholsterer
_____	_____	_____	Assembler, garment
_____	_____	_____	Sewing machine operator
_____	_____	_____	Tailor/dressmaker
_____	_____	_____	Garment inspector
_____	_____	_____	Finisher, Hand

MACHINE TRADE

Next 5 Job	10 Years	Years	Occupation
_____	_____	_____	Machinist
_____	_____	_____	Tool and die maker
_____	_____	_____	Grinder operator
_____	_____	_____	Milling machine set-up
_____	_____	_____	Boring machine operator
_____	_____	_____	Punch press operator
_____	_____	_____	Forming machine operator
_____	_____	_____	Automobile mechanic
_____	_____	_____	Air conditioning mechanic
_____	_____	_____	Maintenance mechanic
_____	_____	_____	Flight engineer
_____	_____	_____	Airframe and powerplant mechanic
_____	_____	_____	Farm equipment mechanic
_____	_____	_____	Diesel mechanic
_____	_____	_____	Small engine mechanic
_____	_____	_____	Machine repair
_____	_____	_____	Office machine service
_____	_____	_____	Environmental construction system installer
_____	_____	_____	Maintenance mechanic
_____	_____	_____	Millwright
_____	_____	_____	Maintenance mechanic helper
_____	_____	_____	Rewinder operator

STRUCTURAL WORK

Next Job	5 Years	10 Years	Occupation
_____	_____	_____	Sheet metal work
_____	_____	_____	Inspector, assembly
_____	_____	_____	Engine assembler
_____	_____	_____	Automobile assembler
_____	_____	_____	Auto body repairer
_____	_____	_____	Shipyard laborer
_____	_____	_____	Welder
_____	_____	_____	Telephone mechanic
_____	_____	_____	Electrician
_____	_____	_____	Painter
_____	_____	_____	Plasterer
_____	_____	_____	Cement mason
_____	_____	_____	Bricklayer
_____	_____	_____	Carpenter
_____	_____	_____	Pipefitter
_____	_____	_____	Plumber
_____	_____	_____	Roofer

MISCELLANEOUS

Next Job	5 Years	10 Years	Occupation
_____	_____	_____	Packager
_____	_____	_____	Bridge crane operator
_____	_____	_____	Power plant operator
_____	_____	_____	Photograph finisher
_____	_____	_____	Printer operator
_____	_____	_____	Other: _____
_____	_____	_____	_____

EXERCISE 5-3: EMERGING FIELDS AND OCCUPATIONS

An emerging occupation can be defined simply as one that no one used to work at, that a few people work at now, and that lots of people will work at in the future. Generally these new occupations are due to technological development or restructuring of existing occupations.

If you wish to learn more about job requirements, projected demand, salary expectations, and other related information, begin your research project by going to a public library and checking a few reference books. Again, acquaint yourself thoroughly with the *Occupational Outlook Handbook* and the *Dictionary of Occupational Titles*. Also look for your state's annual or quarterly report, published by your State Department of Labor or Employment. It provides information on job demand for the state as well as for individual geographic labor markets. You should become familiar with your state's computerized data banks or occupational information systems. They can provide current local job listings as well as national trends and outlooks.

Instructions

Place a check under "Next Job," "5 Years," and/or "10 Years," as you've done in the previous exercises.

Next Job	5 Years	10 Years	Occupation
_____	_____	_____	Child advocate
_____	_____	_____	Crystal manufacturing occupations
_____	_____	_____	Energy efficiency technician
_____	_____	_____	Halfway house resident manager
_____	_____	_____	Horticultural therapy aid
_____	_____	_____	Housing rehabilitation specialist
_____	_____	_____	Industrial hygiene technician
_____	_____	_____	Nuclear quality assurance inspector

_____ _____ _____ Physical security technician

_____ _____ _____ Podiatric assistant

_____ _____ _____ Public safety
communications operator

_____ _____ _____ Case manager for the
mentally disabled

_____ _____ _____ Energy-related occupations

_____ _____ _____ Housing rehabilitation specialist

_____ _____ _____ Laser/electro-optics technician

_____ _____ _____ Microprocessor-related occupations

_____ _____ _____ Tumor registrar

_____ _____ _____ Clinical arrival technician

_____ _____ _____ Computer-assisted design worker

_____ _____ _____ Computer-assisted
manufacturing worker

_____ _____ _____ Deep sea diving and
life support technician

_____ _____ _____ Dialysis technician

_____ _____ _____ Fiber optics worker

_____ _____ _____ Geriatric and
Gerontological technician

_____ _____ _____ Histological technician

_____ _____ _____ Robotics occupations

_____ _____ _____ Surgical technician

_____ _____ _____ Therapeutic recreation technician

EXERCISE 5–4: IDENTIFYING WHERE YOU WORK

Where do you currently work in your organization? Identify that level by placing a check in the left-hand column. In the right-hand column, indicate your top three preferences (1, 2, 3) for your future career planning.

Current Job		Next Job	5 Years	10 Years
____	Top-level manager	____	____	____
____	Middle manager	____	____	____
____	Second-line manager	____	____	____
____	First-line manager/white collar	____	____	____
____	First-line manager/blue collar	____	____	____
____	Technician	____	____	____
____	Staff specialist	____	____	____
____	Professional	____	____	____
____	Secretarial/clerical	____	____	____
____	Operator: _____	____	____	____
____	Other: _____	____	____	____
____	_____	____	____	____
____	_____	____	____	____
____	_____	____	____	____
____	_____	____	____	____

Regionally, where do you want to work in the future? Rank order these alternatives:

_____	Remain at current location	_____	Southwest
_____	Northeast	_____	West
_____	Southeast	_____	International
_____	Midwest		

My short-range (1–2 years) career goals are:

- Preferred industry _____
- Job function/occupation _____
- Realistic organizational level _____
- Geographic preference _____

Summarize this information into a goal statement like: "I want to be working in the high-technology industry as a systems analyst in five years. I realistically can start as a computer programmer in my next job, and I would like to be doing that in the northeastern part of this country."

Summary Statement

_____

_____

_____

_____

_____

My long-range (3–10 years) career goals are:

- Preferred industry _____
- Job function/occupation _____
- Realistic organization level _____
- Geographic preference _____

Summary Statement

_____

_____

_____

_____

_____

EXERCISE 5–6: CAREER/LIFE LINE

Purpose

This and the next exercise help you to delineate your career goals. They also illustrate that career/job goals are not totally separate from your personal and family life. Exercise 5–7, Work/Life Analysis and Planning, is a more precise delineation and plan of this exericse. Both strategies confront you with the reality of a scarce major resource—your own time. Simply stated, the fact is that you have only so many years, but you do have a choice as to how you will spend them. As a result of completing these plans, you will have a greater sense of control over your career/life, and the necessary action steps will become clear. Before you begin this exercise, review the exercises in Chapters 3 and 4.

Instructions

1. The horizontal line in the chart in Figure 5–2 represents your life.
   - On the extreme left side above roman numeral I, write the year you were born.
   - On the extreme right-hand side of the line, write the year you think you will die. Dying may be a difficult issue for you, but it is a certainty. Assume that you will die from natural causes and not as a result of an untimely or accidental death. One way to arrive at this year is to take the average years your grandparents or great-grandparents lived. Calculate the average age, add it to your birthdate, and write down the approximate year.
   - Somewhere between the two points, indicate the current year. Is it one-third, one-half, three quarters of the line?
2. At roman numeral II, below the line, write a few words that illustrate the 5 to 7 major life goals you consciously set out to accomplish and have achieved. You may want to refer to your accomplishments from page 47.

FIGURE 5–2
CAREER/LIFE LINE

IV. Completed Career/Job Goals   *V. Future Career/Job Goals*

I.

_____

II. Completed Life Goals   *III. Future Life Goals*

3. At III, again below the line, write a few words that outline five to seven major future life goals. These should not yet have been accomplished. They should be things that, if you looked back on your entire life when you are approaching death, you could say that, "My life has been worthwhile and satisfying; I accomplished what I set out to do."

4. At IV, above the line, synthesize the five to seven major career goals that you have achieved to date. You may refer to your career progression chart.

5. At V, again above the line, outline your five to seven major future career goals. You deal with your retirement date in this section. Will it be mandatory at 70? Will you take it earlier? Or don't you plan on retiring? Will you develop a second career? What would you like the last position in your career path to be? What are the kinds of positions you will need as steppingstones between now and then? Do you plan on changing careers every ten years? What kinds of careers would you like to have? Perhaps you have two or three alternate career paths.

Reflection and summary

1. What or who has influenced the shape of your "completed" lives?

_____

_____

_____

2. Do you like what you see? _____ Yes _____ No

3. What are some barriers that you will have to deal with to have your desired future take place?

● _____

● _____

● _____

4. What is the probability that your expected future patterns will take place?

Almost   Completely
____ Certain ____ High ____ Medium ____ Low ____ Uncertain

5. What do you have to do to increase the probabilities that your expected future patterns become a reality? Write out a brief action plan.

Action Plan   *When to Start*

● _____

   _____

● _____

   _____

● _____

   _____

EXERCISE 5–7: LIFE/WORK ANALYSIS PLAN

Purpose

A continuation of the last exercise, this section clarifies what you want to make happen in the future. It's a road map or a proposal for your future work history. Remember the old adage, "If you don't know where you're going, any road will take you there." Even if your immediate short-term goal is reemployment, you should consider your long-range goals also. You should make certain that your short-term actions support and develop where you want to be five to ten years from now.

Goals have two characteristics: They should be realistic and measurable. It is realistic to think through the major predictable issues that you will most likely face in your lifetime, as well as when they will take place.

Instructions

Under each of the four categories in the left-hand column (Personal, Career, Family, Retirement) in Figure 5–3, outline your short- and long-range goals.

Each vertical line on the Life/Work Analysis Plan represents one year, with the bold line on the left being the current year. Indicate the estimated time that it will take to accomplish each goal by using a horizontal line between the years.

FIGURE 5–3
LIFE/WORK ANALYSIS PLAN

Year							
Personal goals:							
Career goals:							
Family goals:							
Retirement goals:							
Age							
Company service							
Year							

FIGURE 5-4

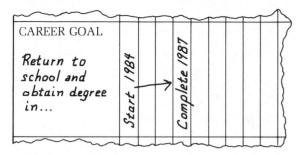

Show start and completion dates, as the example in Figure 5–4 demonstrates. Use the following list to stimulate your thinking:

- Financing education of family members
- Change job/career
- Eliminate major debts
- Move to another area in country/world
- Plan children's wedding

- Start your own business
- Purchase a new home
- Remodel existing home
- Travel extensively
- Take care of and support parents/in-laws

EXERCISE 5–8: LIFE PLANNING ACTION PLAN

Purpose

After illustrating your needs, wants, and desired goals for yourself, your career, your family, and your retirement, you need an Action Plan to implement it.

Instructions

In the chart below, identify the specific actions you can take, as well as the target dates for beginning these actions.

	Action Plan	Starting Target Dates
1.	_____	_____
	_____	_____

	Action Plan	*Starting Target Dates*

2. _____   _____

   _____   _____

3. _____   _____

   _____   _____

4. _____   _____

   _____   _____

5. _____   _____

   _____   _____

6. _____   _____

   _____   _____

7. _____   _____

   _____   _____

Review date for action plan   _____

Person to review plan with   _____

EXERCISE 5–9: CAREER ANALYSIS SUMMARY

Purpose

For the past three chapters, you have been analyzing many aspects of your background—your values, motives, skill clusters, employment history patterns, short- and long-term career/life goals. The following Career Analysis Summary is meant to bring all these sections of the assessment process together so that you can see yourself as a whole, integrated person.

Instructions

After recording the information from the summary sections in Chapters 3, 4, and 5, you should see many aspects of your background begin to overlap and mesh. Your values and work motives may be similar. You may find that you can document them historically by your employment patterns. Your skill clusters may be supported by your employment patterns and values. Your future career/life goals may flow from all these segments. Study this summary before you begin to write the first draft of your resume in Chapter 9.

Personal/Career Values

1. _____
2. _____
3. _____
4. _____
5. _____
6. _____
7. _____
8. _____
9. _____
10. _____

Significant Work Motivators

1. _____
2. _____
3. _____
4. _____
5. _____
6. _____
7. _____
8. _____
9. _____
10. _____

Employment History Patterns

1. _____
2. _____
3. _____
4. _____
5. _____
6. _____
7. _____
8. _____
9. _____
10. _____

Preferred Work Environments

1. _____
2. _____
3. _____
4. _____
5. _____
6. _____
7. _____
8. _____
9. _____
10. _____

Major Skill Clusters	Documentation of Skills
1. _____	_____
2. _____	_____
3. _____	_____
4. _____	_____
5. _____	_____
6. _____	_____
7. _____	_____
8. _____	_____
9. _____	_____
10. _____	_____

Preferred Industry/Organizational Type	Job Function
1. _____	1. _____
2. _____	2. _____
3. _____	3. _____
4. _____	4. _____

Organizational Level

1. _____	2. _____
3. _____	4. _____

Education Background

Degrees	Continuing Education
1. _____	1. _____
2. _____	2. _____
3. _____	3. _____
4. _____	4. _____

References for Further Reading

Bolles, Richard A. *Three Boxes of Life*. Berkeley, Cal.: Ten Speed Press, 1978.

————. *What Color is Your Parachute?* Berkeley, Cal.: Ten Speed Press, 1980.

Burack, Elmer H. and Nicholas Mathys. *Career Management in Organizations: A Practical Human Resources Planning Approach*. Lake Forest, Ill.: Brace Park Press, 1980.

Department of Labor, U.S., *Dictionary of Occupational Titles*, 4th ed. Washington, D.C.: 1977.

Hagberg, Janet and Richard Leider. *The Inventurers*. Reading, Mass.: Addison-Wesley Publishing Company, 1978.

Sheehy, Gail. *Passages*. New York: Bantam Books, 1976.

Simon, Sidney B. *et al. Values Clarification*. New York: Hart, 1972.

Storey, Walter B. *Career Dimensions I*. Croton-on-Hudson, N.Y.: General Electric, 1976.

Terkel, Studs. *Working*. Pantheon Books, 1972.

6

Relocating for a new job

A decision to relocate must be based on sound motivation and a thorough consideration of all factors. The important elements in any successful decision making—communication, research, and the ability to see the implications of alternative decisions—are essential in such a major undertaking as relocation.

Our discussion on relocation includes both job search methods in new areas and the personal/family decision-making process. Yet because relocation decisions are so personal, complex, and subject to such a variety of influences, it is difficult to establish guidelines regarding the sequence of a relocation decision. The following strategy, however, may help you to clarify your options regarding relocation. Rank order each option, letting 1 be the one you consider first, 2 the second, and so on.

Relocation Strategies

_____ Seek employment locally and consider relocation only to _____ area after three months.

_____ Explore relocation to _____ area for first three months and then seek employment locally.

_____ Look locally and at the same time establish long-distance contacts for potential relocation.

_____ Consider the relocation option only after having exhausted all local possibilities.

_____ Relocation is not an alternative for reemployment.

If you decide to relocate, it is critical that you (and your spouse/friend) visit the area, preferably several times and at different times of the year. Look at living conditions, costs, taxes (local and state), schools (if needed), recreational facilities, commuting/transportation, and cost of living. Often higher salaries are negated by higher local consumer costs.

EXERCISE 6–1: LONG-DISTANCE CAMPAIGN ACTIVITIES OVERVIEW

The planning and research for a long-distance campaign usually requires six to eight weeks.

- Identify the preferred geographic area, such as Dallas, Houston, Los Angeles.
- Determine the job opportunity climate of area (Bureau of Labor-Statistics, classified ads).
- Begin your contact file with 3×5 cards stating the following information:
    Name
    Title—functional person in your area of expertise
    Company name
    Address
    City/state/zip
    Phone number
    Product lines
- Subscribe to or pick up at local newsstands the area Sunday newspaper for the classified ads.
- Write a letter to the Executive Secretary of the local Chamber of Commerce requesting specific information, such as:
    Economic climate and job opportunities
    Apartment directories/housing directories from real estate companies
    Maps of the area
    Lists of employment agencies
    Major companies for leads and contacts
- Send 75 to 100 approach letters, allow at least three weeks for replies, and anticipate a 20- to 25-percent response).

- Send a thank-you letter to each response as soon as you receive it; zero in on those expressing interest. Expect negative responses.

- Once you have decided to make a trip to the area, send a decision letter to those expressing interest, stating when you will be in the area, where you will be staying, where you can be called, and when you will call to set up an appointment. If possible, have a local address and phone number on your resume.

- To maximize time, plan your two weeks in the area by grouping appointments into the same geographical area. It is important to have a city/area map.

- Prior to leaving, set up your first three or four appointments for Monday afternoon and Tuesday morning.

- Use any downtime by visiting employment agencies and doing "walk-in interviews" with anyone who is willing to see you.

- Write thank-you letters immediately after the day's interviews.

- Keep accurate notes on names, how interviews went, leads from interviews, any planned follow-ups, using page 199.

Job search

How do you set up a marketing campaign in an area where you have no contacts? First, identify one or two specific areas (locations). Then:

- Subscribe to the Sunday editions of the area newspapers for eight to twelve weeks. Carefully check the classified sections as well as the Business and Local sections to become acquainted with the local business climate.

- Write to the area chamber of commerce for information, including maps of the area, or lists of employment agencies, major industries, and business organizations.

- Speak with family, business associates, college alumni, friends, and acquaintances in the area who might be helpful to you in your job search.

- Go to your local library and research approximately 100 major companies in the area you are considering for relocation. Use the geographical index (yellow section) of

Volume III, Indexes of Standard and Poor's *Directory of Corporations, Directors, and Executives*. Record relevant organizational data from Volume I on 3×5 cards, including:

Name
Title
Organization
Address   Telephone
Product lines

- Write a concise letter to the person in the organization asking for information and help. Identify the person by name and title. Do not ask for a job. State you are considering a major move to the area and are seeking this persons judgement of the business and employment climate for someone with your background. Outline your qualifications in two or three sentences. Ask whether it would be wise to make a personal visit to the area and look around, or would it be better to send a number of resumes to companies that may result in advance job possibilities? Express your appreciation for his/her opinion, and state that you look forward to hearing from him/her. If the letter is not on your own printed stationery, be sure that your address and phone number are included. (See the sample letter in Figure 6–1.)

- Respond briefly and immediately to replies with a thank you and "I'll keep you informed."

- If you are encouraged by your research findings, plan a trip to the area. Allow at least two weeks of active job searching. Because the trip entails an out-of-pocket cost, you need to plan your time and budget your money carefully.

- Mail a letter to each of your original respondents, stating that you will be in the area on a given date and that you are looking forward to thanking them in person for their advice. Enclose a copy of your resume, which they "could pass along in case they hear of a job opening that would be appropriate."

- Using the appointment schedule in Figure 6–2, make phone calls immediately upon arriving in the area to set up appointments. More than half your calls should result in interviews.

FIGURE 6–1
SAMPLE RELOCATION INQUIRY LETTER

Mr. James Smith
184 Main Street
Anywhere, California   97214

Dear Mr. Smith:

I am doing some market research before making the major decision whether or not to move to _____ and would appreciate your help.

Since _____ is your area of expertise I am sure you are very aware of the employment climate for _____. My current job as _____ has included: (state job responsibilities). I am interested in continuing my career in this field and am anxious to know your comments on the possibilities of employment in _____ for a person with my background.

Any information or direction you could share will be most helpful to me in making a sound and realistic decision about relocating and establishing my career in the _____ area.

       Sincerely,   _____

- Often employers are reluctant to hire out-of-towners, so try to establish a temporary local address before you begin your job campaign. Your address might be with a friend, relative, temporary apartment, or local motel/hotel (frequently you can negotiate a good weekly/monthly rate).

FIGURE 6–2
LONG-DISTANCE CAMPAIGN APPOINTMENT SCHEDULE

First Week	Monday	Tuesday	Wednesday	Thursday	Friday	Saturday
9:00 am	Call & set appointments for the first week.					
10:30 am						
1:00 pm						
3:30 pm						
Evenings	Send thank-you letters/review day/keep detailed notes					
Second Week						
9:00 am						
10:30 am						
1:00 pm						
3:30 pm						
Evenings						

EXERCISE 6–2: RELOCATION DECISIONS

Faced with the relocation issue, you must make a set of decisions with a degree of uncertainty. People think nothing of spending six months to plan a vacation or a year to search for the right house, but they often decide overnight to relocate. Whether you are a one-wage-earner family or a two-career household, relocation can be traumatic.

Whether you plan to relocate at your own expense or your new employer is offering assistance, the following items are major financial considerations:

- Home search counseling service
- Home search expenses (for spouse or other family member)
- Interim living expenses (for employee)
- Temporary commutation expenses
- Home sale plan
- New home closing costs
- Mortgage loan fee
- Equity advance (current homeowner only)
- Lease penalties and loss of security deposits
- Shipment of household goods
- Days-of-move expenses
- Miscellaneous expense allowance
- Cash advance
- Special housing allowance

The following decision-making techniques do not make your decisions for you—only you can do that. The approach helps you to clarify the major factors, consequences, and outcomes in the relocation decision by quantifying the uncertainties. This method assesses the costs and benefits associated with relocation decisions. First, assign your own subjective probability that the event will happen. Let 1.0 equal 100-percent probability and 0.0 no likelihood at all. To assign a probability, guess at the likelihood of certain outcomes based on a particular decision. To each consequence you also assign a value that reflects the importance of the outcome to you. Let 10 represent the greatest importance and 0 no importance. To arrive at an expectancy value, multiply the probability by the value. Do the same for each consequence and add up the expected values of all the consequences. After completing each set of major alternatives, the total expected values are compared for each set of choices.

Let's examine an example in which a person has to decide whether to relocate or to reject an offer from another area. First, list all the possible factors and consequences associated with each major decision as shown in Figure 6–3a. After listing all the consequences of that decision, the person in the example assigned absolute certainty that the first consequence would happen (probability = 1.0). Then the person does the same for the decision to reject the offer. Comparing both decisions, the rejection decision has a slightly higher expected value (27.1 versus 24.7), indicating that it may be the preferred choice. Generally speaking, the decision with the highest expected value is the preferred decision. You must, however, examine the trade-offs. The new relocated position is pre-

FIGURE 6–3a

DECISION 1: TO ACCEPT THE NEW POSITION IN A NEW LOCATION

Consequences	Probability	× Value	= Expected Value
I will have a job.	1.0	10	10.0
There are average schools.	0.5	6	3.0
I will not have to commute.	0.9	9	8.1
Spouse will be looking for job.	0.4	9	3.6
Total expected value of decision			24.7

FIGURE 6–3b

DECISION 2: TO REJECT THE OFFER OF A POSITION IN A NEW LOCATION

Consequences	Probability	× Value	= Expected Value
I will not have a job in near future.	0.9	10	9.0
Schools here are excellent.	1.0	0	9.0
Spouse will have job.	1.0	9	9.0
I'll have to keep job hunting.	1.0	1	.01
Total expected value of decision			27.1

ferred to a continuing search, but the trade-off of your spouse's job may need further information and discussion. Are your spouse's skills easily marketable in the new area? What would he/she be giving up in order to make the move?

At best, analyzing these decisions is a subjective guessing game. You can never have perfect information. As you get more information, your expected values may change, and the information could provide you with a clearer set of choices.

FIGURE 6–4

RELOCATION DECISION WORKSHEET: JOB ITSELF [SELF]*

Decision: _____

Possible Consequences	Probability	Value	Expected Value
Professional identity	____	____	____
Professional/career/business contacts	____	____	____
Job Security	____	____	____
Salary level	____	____	____
Rate of salary increments	____	____	____
Quality of the organization	____	____	____
Quality of the position	____	____	____
Colleagues	____	____	____
Work environment and facilities	____	____	____
Future career opportunities and job advancement	____	____	____
Other:			
_____	____	____	____
_____	____	____	____
_____	____	____	____
_____	____	____	____
_____	____	____	____

Total expected value   ____

*The Relocation Decision Worksheets on this and the following pages are adapted from F. Hall and D. Hall, *The Two-Career Couple* © 1979, Addison-Wesley, Reading, Massachusetts. Reprinted with permission.

Figures 6–4 through 6–10 provide you with two sets of worksheets, one for you and one for your spouse/friend. There are separate worksheets for assessing the job itself, lifestyle and family factors, and for personal and individual factors. All these worksheets should be completed separately for each area. Compare and discuss them. Add as many consequences as you feel necessary to thoroughly explore each set of choices.

FIGURE 6–5

RELOCATION DECISION WORKSHEET: LIFE STYLE AND FAMILY FACTORS [SELF]

Decision: _____

Possible consequences	Probability	Value	Expected Value
Geographic location	_____	_____	_____
Living areas accessible to work	_____	_____	_____
Types of housing available	_____	_____	_____
Neighborhoods (you can afford)	_____	_____	_____
Transportation	_____	_____	_____
Schools	_____	_____	_____
Shopping	_____	_____	_____
Cultural facilities	_____	_____	_____
Recreational facilities	_____	_____	_____
Local social norms and attitudes	_____	_____	_____
Cost of living/unusual expenses	_____	_____	_____
Sports	_____	_____	_____
Local government/politics	_____	_____	_____
Community organizations	_____	_____	_____
Baby-sitters/day-care facilities	_____	_____	_____
Household help	_____	_____	_____
Restaurants	_____	_____	_____
Churches/synagogues	_____	_____	_____
Social relationships/friends	_____	_____	_____
Family/relatives	_____	_____	_____
Media/communications	_____	_____	_____

Total expected value   _____

FIGURE 6–6
RELOCATION DECISION WORKSHEET: PERSONAL AND INDIVIDUAL FACTORS [SELF]

Decision: _____

Possible Consequences	Probability	Value	Expected Value
Unique personal losses or gains involved in the choice	_____	_____	_____
Giving up old friends	_____	_____	_____
Energy required to make the move	_____	_____	_____
Emotional costs of readjusting to job changes	_____	_____	_____
Emotional costs of adjusting to new social relationships	_____	_____	_____
Emotional costs of integrating self into new neighborhood	_____	_____	_____
Emotional costs of integrating children into new schools	_____	_____	_____
Emotional costs of changes in family relationships	_____	_____	_____
Anxiety about proving self in new job or environment	_____	_____	_____
Excitement of new opportunities in new location	_____	_____	_____
Other: _____	_____	_____	_____
_____	_____	_____	_____
_____	_____	_____	_____
_____	_____	_____	_____
_____	_____	_____	_____
_____	_____	_____	_____

Total expected value _____

FIGURE 6–7

Decision: _____

Possible Consequences	Probability	Value	Expected Value
Professional identity	_____	_____	_____
Professional/career/business contacts	_____	_____	_____
Job security	_____	_____	_____
Salary level	_____	_____	_____
Rate of salary increments	_____	_____	_____
Quality of the organization	_____	_____	_____
Quality of the position	_____	_____	_____
Colleagues	_____	_____	_____
Work environment and facilities	_____	_____	_____
Future career opportunities and job advancement	_____	_____	_____
Other:			
_____	_____	_____	_____
_____	_____	_____	_____
_____	_____	_____	_____
_____	_____	_____	_____
_____	_____	_____	_____
_____	_____	_____	_____
_____	_____	_____	_____
_____	_____	_____	_____

Total expected value _____

FIGURE 6–8

Decision: _____

Possible Consequences	Probability	Value	Expected Value
Geographic location	_____	_____	_____
Living areas accessible to work	_____	_____	_____
Types of housing available	_____	_____	_____
Neighborhoods (you can afford)	_____	_____	_____
Transportation	_____	_____	_____
Schools	_____	_____	_____
Shopping	_____	_____	_____
Cultural facilities	_____	_____	_____
Recreational facilities	_____	_____	_____
Local social norms and attitudes	_____	_____	_____
Cost of living/unusual expenses	_____	_____	_____
Sports	_____	_____	_____
Local government/politics	_____	_____	_____
Community organizations	_____	_____	_____
Baby-sitters/day-care facilities	_____	_____	_____
Household help	_____	_____	_____
Restaurants	_____	_____	_____
Churches/synagogues	_____	_____	_____
Social relationships/friends	_____	_____	_____
Family/relatives	_____	_____	_____
Media/communications	_____	_____	_____
Total expected value			_____

FIGURE 6–9

Decision: _____

Possible Consequences	Probability	Value	Expected Value
Unique personal losses or gains involved in the choice	_____	_____	_____
Giving up old friends	_____	_____	_____
Energy required to make the move	_____	_____	_____
Emotional costs of readjusting to job changes	_____	_____	_____
Emotional costs of adjusting to new social relationships	_____	_____	_____
Emotional costs of integrating self into new neighborhood	_____	_____	_____
Emotional costs of integrating children into new schools	_____	_____	_____
Emotional costs of changes in family relationships	_____	_____	_____
Anxiety about proving self in new job or environment	_____	_____	_____
Excitement of new opportunities in new location	_____	_____	_____
Other: _____	_____	_____	_____
_____	_____	_____	_____
_____	_____	_____	_____
_____	_____	_____	_____
_____	_____	_____	_____

Total expected value   _____

FIGURE 6–10
RELOCATION DECISION SUMMARY SHEET

My tentative decision: _____

_____

_____

_____

_____

My family's tentative decision(s): _____

_____

_____

_____

_____

Things that need further discussion and investigation:

_____

_____

_____

_____

_____

_____

Date to make final decision: _____

References for Further Reading

Hall, Francine S. and Douglas T. Hall. *The Two Career Couple*. Reading, Mass.: Addison-Wesley Publishing Company, 1979. Especially Chapter 9.

Brown, Rex V. *et al. Decision Analysis: An Overview*. New York: Holt, Rinehart, & Winston, 1974.

Raymond, Ronald J. and Stephen V. Eliot. *Grow Your Roots Anywhere, Anytime*. New York: Peter H. Wyden, Inc., Publisher, 1980.

7

Looking at
early retirement as an option

Perhaps you have not considered early retirement feasible, but at times it presents another career alternative. Even if you are suddenly faced with the possibility of an unexpected "early retirement," it is wise to take some time to think through the major issues and to do some planning.

What is retirement? The whole concept of retirement is relatively new. Only in the last couple of decades has retirement come to be universally accepted. In 1950, 46 percent of the men in the country over 65 were still in the labor force. By 1970, only 25 percent of them over 65 were still working. Actually, retirement can occur at almost any age, and it is just one stage within a person's life career development. As in all life stages, retirement provides the opportunity to make a choice from available options. Yet most people don't know—and avoid finding out—what retirement is all about until it is upon them.

Retirement—whether voluntary, involuntary, early, special early, or however—entails the same opportunities, options, and problems.

- What are you going to do with your time?
- How are you going to arrange your lifestyle?
- How are you going to handle the mechanics of your new status—finance, health, housing, family needs, personal needs?

Out of the spotty retirement research to date, the only conclusive fact is an overwhelming consensus that those who plan their retirement are living fuller and happier lives than those who do not. For the majority of retired persons, the most pressing need is to be useful—to do something that provides personal recognition. We do not mean to understate the real need to deal with the necessary financial, health, housing, and legal aspects of retirement. Yet equally important, and often more so, are the changes in lifestyle, in activities, in handling stress, in dealing with myths on aging, in marital communications, and in adjusting to a new life stage. Managing the retirement transition, in whatever form the change takes requires planning. While being flexible is important, detailed and specific plans yield the best results. Planning gives us the ability to direct and control our retirement, rather than just reacting to our circumstances.

EXERCISE 7–1: PERSONAL EXPECTATIONS IN RETIREMENT

Very often, what you expect is what you get. Be realistic: Your behavior and interest patterns do not readily change. How do you approach the idea of retirement? How will you feel about your new status? How will it affect your personality? How do you expect to satisfy the psychological needs that your career provided, such as self-respect, prestige, respect of others, sociability, enjoyment, service to others, leisure? These needs are real, and they do not change because you are retired. What do change are the means of satisfying these needs. To find alternative ways of meeting these needs, you must know yourself and know your personal goals for this new life stage. You may discover that your given needs have new priorities, some of which are less important, and some of which are more important than those in your working career.

What is important to you now? To answer this question, rank the following items from 1 to 15:

_____ To be recognized in the community?

_____ To work with a well-known company or institution?

_____ To see the results of my efforts?

_____ To learn from what I do?

_____ To do something
useful?

_____ To use my leader-
ship abilities?

_____ To have a title?

_____ To help others?

_____ To try out my own
ideas?

_____ To test myself?

_____ To make a lot of
money?

_____ To be self-reliant?

_____ To work with con-
genial people?

_____ To tackle problems
and find solutions?

_____ To remain active?

Once you identify these personal motivations, you can more
readily find a direction to best meet your personal needs.

Now complete these open-ended statements to clarify
your thinking/feelings about retirement:

The biggest challenge retirement poses to me is learning to _____
_____
_____

The part of retirement I am most looking forward to is _____
_____
_____

I will find it difficult to let go of _____
_____
_____

I'm planning to start _____
_____
_____

Most people I know who have retired _____
_____
_____

My friends think my reaction to retirement will be _____
_____
_____

I'm afraid of retiring because _____

_____

_____

Retirement will provide an opportunity to _____

_____

_____

_____

_____

Reviewing these completed statements with your spouse/friend can give you a better perspective on your actual reaction to retirement.

EXERCISE 7–2: FINANCIAL PLANNING AND LEGAL AFFAIRS

Financial planning is probably the keystone of retirement planning. It is certainly the first area to deal with since so much of retirement planning depends on your financial resources. The Bureau of Labor Statistics estimates that the "average" retired couple has a budget similar to the following:

Housing	33.6%
Food and beverages	27.7%
Goods and services	13.6%
Clothing	8.9%
Transportation	8.9%
Medical care	7.3%

How does your budget compare? To anticipate and plan for change in your standard of living, consider completing the financial planning worksheets in Figures 7–1 and 7–2. This detailed breakdown should give you some idea of any adjustments and/or changes that you may need to make in your lifestyle. The amount of your net worth is not important. What is important is whether that amount allows you to live the lifestyle you planned, as well as whether it meets your needs for financial security.

FIGURE 7–1

RETIREMENT FINANCIAL PLANNING WORKSHEETS

Item	Monthly Expenses Present Cost	Anticipated Retirement Costs
Housing	$_____	$_____
Food	_____	_____
Clothing	_____	_____
Medical care	_____	_____
Transportation	_____	_____
Savings	_____	_____
Taxes	_____	_____
Personal and miscellaneous	_____	_____
Recreation	_____	_____
Home maintenance	_____	_____
Total	$_____	$_____

Source	Monthly Income Present	Anticipated Retirement Income
Salary	$_____	$_____
Pension	_____	_____
Social Security	_____	_____
Savings accounts	_____	_____
Bonds and preferred stocks	_____	_____
Common stocks and investment trusts	_____	_____
Life insurance	_____	_____
Real estate	_____	_____
Other sources	_____	_____
Total	$_____	$_____

FIGURE 7–2

Assets		Liabilities	
Bank Balance	$ _____	Accounts due	$ _____
Cash value of insurance	_____	Notes due	_____
Market value of real estate	_____	Mortgages owned	_____
Cash value of business	_____	Debts	_____
Cash value of automobile	_____	Claims against your	
Cash value of household		estate	_____
furnishings	_____	Unpaid taxes	_____
Social security benefits	_____	Other	_____
Annuities and pensions	_____		_____
Market value of stocks and bonds	_____		_____
Notes receivable	_____		_____
Accounts receivable	_____		_____
Other	_____		
	_____		
Total assets	_____	Total liabilities	$ _____
Subtract your liabilities from your assets to get your net worth			$ _____

Financial planning should also include a careful organization of all your papers:

- Deed to your house
- Title of ownership paper
- Life insurance policies
- Social security cards
- Cancelled checks (for three years, seven for tax purposes)

- Securities
- Your will
- Records of investments
- Receipts

Also, organize your estate. Yes, you have one. The federal government imposes a tax on estates over $60,000, and many states have their own inheritance or estate taxes.

Here's an income-saving technique to ease the transition to retirement. Keep track of all your expenses over one year. The following year, make a goal of cutting the weekly budget by $10 and thus saving $500. The next year, the objective is to cut $20 from the weekly budget, saving $1,000. By the fifth year, you are saving at a rate of $4,500 a year, and you have a total savings of $7,500 (plus interest)—as well as having learned to live on a lower income!

Another way to ease the transition is to practice living on your retirement income for a one- or two-year period. Miscalculations in your budget show up quickly, and they can then be corrected before they do too much damage.

If you need assistance with your financial planning, local professional sources can give it: county extension services, family service agencies, some credit unions, and savings and loan associations. Also check with your local senior citizens center. Frequently, community colleges and universities offer continuing education programs in finance planning.

EXERCISE 7–3: NEW CAREER OPPORTUNITIES

The possibilities for a new career at this time are considerably greater than you might suppose. Older workers have a lot going for them. In a recent study employers gave the following characteristics as those they would value above youth, strength, and agility:

- Adaptability
- Experience
- Dependability
- Good work habits
- Consistent performance
- Knowledge
- Pride in work
- Stability

All in all, a pretty accurate description of an older worker!

Again, planning and attitude are the key words. When deciding on a new career that is best for you at this stage of your life, think carefully about the kind of person you are, your needs, your desires, your strengths and weaknesses, your abilities, your interests, your experience, and your financial freedom or financial constraints. Working through Chapters 3–5 is helpful in identifying new career opportunities.

Another help when thinking about a new career direction is the following exercise. Allow yourself at least 30 minutes. In a relaxed frame of mind, complete the following sentence:

The perfect job for me would be _____

_____

_____

_____.

If you are completely honest with yourself you may be surprised and pleased with what you have written. Perhaps you should give it some serious thought.

It is particularly important to understand what you want from a new career. Rank order the following motives from 1 to 6.

____ Something to do?   ____ Respect?

____ Status?   ____ A way to get out of the house?

____ Money?   ____ Other?

____ A sense of being useful?

When considering your next career, look at your skills and interests from a new perspective; don't be locked into your old job titles. Put your interests to work for you. Consider part-time work, temporary assignments, regular or occasional commitments, or your own business. Once you decide what you want to do and where you want to do it, your job hunting process is no different from the procedures outlined in Chapters 9 and 10.

Additional employment information sources for older workers are:

- Forty Plus Clubs (executive/management) in major cities
- Retired Persons Association, 1625 I Street, NW, Washington, D.C. 20006

- Mature Temps (in major cities)
- SCORE (Service Corporation of Retired Executives)
- IESC (International Executive Service Corporation)
- Nonprofit employment agencies, such as the local chamber of commerce, YWCA, YMCA, Salvation Army, as well as state employment agencies.

EXERCISE 7–4: HOUSING AND COMMUNITY RESOURCES

Retirement brings with it many choices. In general, retirement obliges you to consider which areas of your lifestyle you want to change and which you want to maintain. Housing, which represents 34 percent of your retirement budget, is such a consideration. Don't jump into something for the sake of making a change—especially when it comes to housing and relocation. Never decide to move on impulse. Don't do it in a hurry, because your friends did or because you think life will be completely different. Move only if and when you really want to.

Your home base is a major factor in determining your other activities. As in all your decisions, a housing decision touches on the kind of lifestyle you want and the kind of person you are. Consider all the alternatives in terms of physical space, economic considerations, relationships with family and friends, your identity (which you might have to reestablish if you move), and, most importantly, *your* wishes regardless of all else. In making this decision, open communication between you and your spouse/friend is of the utmost importance.

Consider the options in the following exercise. Of the six basic housing options that follow, indicate your preference in order of priority. Rank order them from 1 to 6.

Preferences   *Options*

_____   *Stay in my present home:*
               Leave my home base, residence,
               neighborhood, friends, local business
               relationships in tact.

_____   *Move elsewhere in the same community:*
               Find housing more suitable to my present

needs and resources, while keeping a high
degree of stability in my larger life context.

_____ *Move to a new community locally:*
Find housing more suitable to my present needs
and resources.

_____ *Move out of state within the same region:*
Start a new life with the same general climate
but a new set of personal and business affiliations.

_____ *Move to a new region of the country:*
Experience a whole new lifestyle through a
major move to another region of the country, such as
North to South or East to West.

_____ *Move to another country:*
Plunge into a new culture by taking up residence
or actually emigrating to a foreign country.

In setting these priorities, consider the following housing
and living arrangements:

- Home ownership
- Rented housing
- Building a retirement home
- Mobile home
- Retirement Community
- Condominium
- Apartment rental
- Apartment cooperative
- Public housing
- Retirement home
- Residential hotel
- Town house
- Shared housing with friends
- Shared housing with family/children

EXERCISE 7–5: HEALTH AND STRESS IN RETIREMENT

Retirement itself may not produce stress, but as a change,
it requires adjustment and very often adjustments can be
stressful. A study on stress indicates that adjustment to retirement is actually half as stressful as the loss of a spouse.

Your own personal pattern of coping with stress therefore
affects your retirement and your health. Think about how you
cope with stressful situations. Are you pleased, or would you
feel better, if you didn't fly off the handle, or sulk, or whatever? You may not be able to change situations, but you can

change your responses and attitudes toward them. All of us perceive retirement stress differently, and often differently at different times. Some people see retirement as situational, an objective fact; others view it as something being done to them. Which view you take determines how you cope (that attitude again!).

Review all aspects of your physical well-being, including what you eat. With a change in lifestyle, it is especially important to make sure your nutritional needs are being met.

Have you planned adequate exercise? Have you scheduled regular medical checkups? Are you aware of any excess in alcohol comsumption? Do you know about preventive health measures?

Are you aware of the strong relationship between mental and physical well being? There is a strong relationship between a person's mental and physical condition. To cope well, you should be as physically healthy as possible. A Gallup poll of persons 65 and over reported that, of 81 percent with one or more chronic conditions, only 45 percent reported *any* limitation in their activities by the chronic condition. In addition, only 16 percent reported conditions that inhibited major activities.

EXERCISE 7–6: LEISURE AND PERSONAL TIME PLANNING

In retirement, you're suddenly not in charge of anything but yourself. Your established daily routine is gone. Too much unplanned time can lead to boredom, a sense of frustration, and even guilt. Many retirement researchers are convinced that the improper use and nonuse of leisure time are responsible for more emotional problems among retired persons than money or health problems.

You need to channel your work energies into the new business of living well. The external things may change—less money to spend, moving, more time for hobbies, more time for self. These changes help us to determine how we plan our leisure time and how we feel about our own status. To a great extent, our moods are also a determining factor in structuring our leisure.

Can you handle all the free time? A study from Duke University's Center of Aging indicates that over half of 200 men surveyed (52 percent) said that they got more satisfaction from work than they did from leisure. Fifty-five percent of the women surveyed said they enjoyed working more than they enjoyed having free time.

So make demands on yourself. Insist that the leisure activities you choose:

- stimulate you, give you a new zeal,
- are both physically and intellectually stimulating, and
- offer excitement and anticipation.

You need to do more than "be busy." Your retirement goal is therefore to fill your time in a meaningful way. To do so, you need to answer two questions:

1. How do you spend your time?
2. How would you like to spend your time?

The following exercise has two parts. Figure 7–3 is an analysis of how you are currently spending your time, and Figure 7–4 helps you to outline how you would like to spend your time.

Unless you are a single person living alone, it is understood that all these planning activities are joint activities with you and your spouse/friend. This understanding holds whether you are the traditional "bread-winner" husband with a "homemaker" wife or a member of a dual-career family with only one partner retiring. Be careful to avoid solutions that benefit one person at the expense of the other.

Instructions

Figure 7–3 is an inventory of your daily life, that is, how you *actually* spend your time and energy. Estimate the number of hours you spend each day on the following categories. Then draw slices in the pie to proportionately represent each of the following categories:

- sleeping
- eating

- food preparation
- personal appearance

- television
- exercise
- work
- reading
- yard maintenance
- travel

- house maintenance
- hobbies/games
- friends/socializing
- family socializing
- shopping

FIGURE 7–3

Daily life schedule

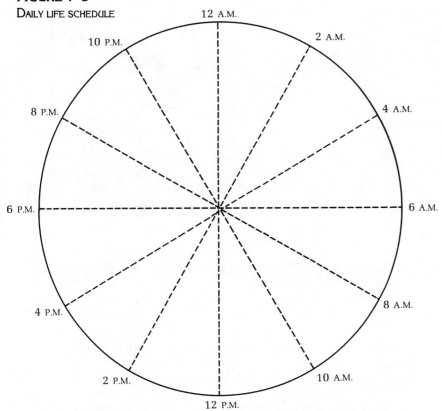

Reprinted by permission of A&W Publishers, Inc. from *Values Clarification: A Handbook of Practical Strategies for Teachers and Students*, New Revised Edition, by Sidney B. Simon, Leland W. Howe, and Howard Kirschenbaum. Copyright © 1972; copyright © 1978. Hart Publishing Company, Inc.

Figure 7–4 is an inventory of how you *would like* to spend your time and energy. Do the same as you did for Figure 7–3.

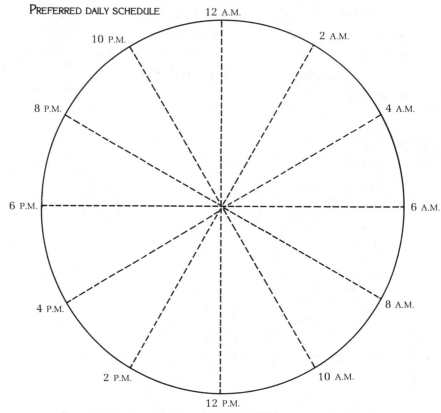

FIGURE 7–4

Preferred daily schedule

12 A.M.

10 P.M.   2 A.M.

8 P.M.   4 A.M.

6 P.M.   6 A.M.

4 P.M.   8 A.M.

2 P.M.   10 A.M.

12 P.M.

Reprinted by permission of A&W Publishers, Inc. from *Values Clarification: A Handbook of Practical Strategies for Teachers and Students*, New Revised Edition, by Sidney B. Simon, Leland W. Howe, and Howard Kirschenbaum. Copyright © 1972; copyright © 1978. Hart Publishing Company, Inc.

Then answer the questions relating to the two figures.

Gaps between daily schedule and preferred schedule

1. What gaps exist between your two schedules?

2. What can you do to change your daily schedule to live more the way you wish?

Action Plan   *Dates*

1. _____   _____

2. _____   _____

3. _____   _____

4. _____ _____

5. _____ _____

6. _____ _____

Given your new lifestyle (and finances), you may want to check your proposed activities against certain criteria: Does the activity provide a complete change of pace? Does it combine general activities? Is it within your budget? Is it within easy distance? Does it offer beginners a sense of accomplishment, develop a skill you already have, and so on? The exercise in Figure 7–5 may help you to organize your evaluation. The list of activities in Figure 7–6 is designed to help you and your spouse/friend determine what you *now* do with your leisure time and what you might prefer doing *more of* in retirement.

FIGURE 7–5
EVALUATION OF ACTIVITIES

Do I like?	Possible Activities	Change of pace	Within budget	Sense of accomplishment	Distance	New Skills	Further Develop Skills
____ to do things alone?							
____ to do things with others?							
____ to do things for fun?							
____ to do things to learn?							
____ to do things for my health?							
____ to do things to become expert?							
____ to do things to earn money?							
____ other reasons?							

Instructions

Read the entire list carefully, and then go back to the beginning and rate each activity according to the following scale:

1 = Never
2 = Rarely
3 = Sometimes
4 = Often
5 = Quite often

Place these numerical ratings in the column headed Now. Then go back again and rate each activity in terms of your desire to do it in the future. Place those responses in the column headed Future. Have your spouse/close friend do the same and place his/her ratings in the appropriate columns. Then:

- Compare the items you rated a "5" in the Future column with the rating you gave the item in the Now column. Are there any changes?

- Compare the items rated a "5" by your spouse with the rating you gave the item in the Now and the Future columns.

- Make a list of the items rated "5" in the Future column, but lower than "5" in the Now column under Self. Specify a date on which you will start doing or doing more of that activity.

- Have your spouse/friend make a list of the items he/she rated "5" in the Future column, but lower than "5" in the Now column under Spouse. Specify the date on which he/she will begin doing or doing more of that activity.

- Finally, make a list of the items that both of you want to do or do more of *together* in the future. For each item, specify a date when you will both start that activity.

---

*Adapted from Jack Bologna's "Leisure Time Satisfaction Scale." Used with permission.

FIGURE 7–6

RETIREMENT LEISURE TIME SATISFACTION SCALE*

	Self		Spouse	
	Now	Future	Now	Future
Attending/viewing/listening				
a. Movie	___	___	___	___
b. Art shows	___	___	___	___
c. Concerts/ballets	___	___	___	___
d. Church services	___	___	___	___
e. Athletic events	___	___	___	___
f. Stage plays	___	___	___	___
g. Lectures	___	___	___	___
h. TV viewing	___	___	___	___
i. Listening to music	___	___	___	___
j. Listening to radio	___	___	___	___
k. Other: _____	___	___	___	___
Collecting				
a. Art work	___	___	___	___
b. Antiques	___	___	___	___
c. Books	___	___	___	___
d. Stamps	___	___	___	___
e. Coins	___	___	___	___
f. Records	___	___	___	___
g. Recipes	___	___	___	___
h. Other: _____	___	___	___	___
Building and construction				
a. Models	___	___	___	___
b. Furniture	___	___	___	___

FIGURE 7–6
(Cont.)

	Self		Spouse	
	Now	*Future*	*Now*	*Future*
c. Toys/playthings	——	——	——	——
d. Remodeling/repairs	——	——	——	——
e. Other: _____	——	——	——	——

Creating/designing/crafting
a. Painting	——	——	——	——
b. Sculpture	——	——	——	——
c. Play acting	——	——	——	——
d. Fiction writing	——	——	——	——
e. Poetry	——	——	——	——
f. Music writing	——	——	——	——
g. Music playing	——	——	——	——
h. Singing	——	——	——	——
i. Dancing	——	——	——	——
j. Home decorating	——	——	——	——
k. Floral design/arranging	——	——	——	——
l. Sewing/knitting/needlepointing	——	——	——	——
m. Pottery/jewelry	——	——	——	——
n. Designing and making clothes	——	——	——	——
o. Other: _____	——	——	——	——

Indoors
a. Cooking	——	——	——	——
b. Dining out	——	——	——	——
c. Entertaining friends	——	——	——	——
d. Playing with children	——	——	——	——
e. Visiting friends/relatives	——	——	——	——
f. Other: _____	——	——	——	——

FIGURE 7–6
(Cont.)

	Self		Spouse	
	Now	Future	Now	Future

Outdoors

a. Camping   ⎯   ⎯   ⎯   ⎯

b. Hiking   ⎯   ⎯   ⎯   ⎯

c. Fishing   ⎯   ⎯   ⎯   ⎯

d. Hunting   ⎯   ⎯   ⎯   ⎯

e. Skiing   ⎯   ⎯   ⎯   ⎯

f. Gardening   ⎯   ⎯   ⎯   ⎯

g. Lawn care   ⎯   ⎯   ⎯   ⎯

h. Trail biking   ⎯   ⎯   ⎯   ⎯

i. Cycling   ⎯   ⎯   ⎯   ⎯

j. Boating/sailing   ⎯   ⎯   ⎯   ⎯

k. Other: _____   ⎯   ⎯   ⎯

Physical exercise

a. Jogging   ⎯   ⎯   ⎯   ⎯

b. Tennis   ⎯   ⎯   ⎯   ⎯

c. Swimming   ⎯   ⎯   ⎯   ⎯

d. Golf   ⎯   ⎯   ⎯   ⎯

e. Handball/paddle ball/racquetball   ⎯   ⎯   ⎯   ⎯

f. Weightlifting   ⎯   ⎯   ⎯   ⎯

g. Walking   ⎯   ⎯   ⎯   ⎯

h. Dancing   ⎯   ⎯   ⎯   ⎯

i. Circuit training   ⎯   ⎯   ⎯   ⎯

j. Other: _____   ⎯   ⎯   ⎯

Playing

a. Card games   ⎯   ⎯   ⎯   ⎯

FIGURE 7–6
(Cont.)

	Self		Spouse	
	Now	Future	Now	Future
b. Board games	—	—	—	—
c. Team sports	—	—	—	—
d. Video/computer games	—	—	—	—
e. Other: _____	—	—	—	—
Intellectualizing				
a. Reading/fiction/poetry	—	—	—	—
b. Reading/nonfiction	—	—	—	—
c. Studying/schooling	—	—	—	—
d. Researching	—	—	—	—
e. Meditating	—	—	—	—
f. Career planning	—	—	—	—
g. Financial planning	—	—	—	—
h. Other: _____	—	—	—	—

	Self	*Date*
1.	_____	_____
2.	_____	_____
3.	_____	_____
4.	_____	_____

	Spouse	*Date*
1.	_____	_____
2.	_____	_____
3.	_____	_____
4.	_____	_____

	Together		Date
1.	_____		_____
2.	_____		_____
3.	_____		_____
4.	_____		_____

References for Further Reading

AARP and NRTA. *Planning for Retirement: A Bibliography of Retirement Planning Literature.* Washington, D.C. [1909 "K" Street, N.W., Washington, D.C. 20049]: 1980.

Bradford, Leland P. and Martha Bradford. *Retirement, Coping with Emotional Upheavals.* Illinois: Nelson-Hall, 1979.

The Future of the Older Worker in America, A Work in America Institute Policy Study. Elmsford, N.Y.: Work in America Institute, Inc., 1980.

Lakein, Alan. *How to Get Control of Your Time and Your Life.* New York: Peter Wyden, Publisher, 1973.

The Older Worker in an Aging Society: A Special Report. Ann Arbor, Mich.: Institute of Gerontology, University of Michigan, 1981.

Uris, Auren. *Over 50.* New York: Bantam Books, 1981.

Weinstein, Grace W. *Life Plans.* New York: Holt, Rinehart, & Winston, 1979.

Willing, Jules Z. *The Reality of Retirement.* New York: William Morrow and Company, Inc., 1981.

8

Making decisions in a two-career family

The two-income, two-career family is one of the fastest growing socio-economic classes in the country, increasing from 12 million in 1960 to more than 25 million in 1981. As a group, these couples are still working out their roles for managing this relatively new household structure.

Today's two-career couples usually think of both careers as equally important. However, a 1981 nation-wide survey conducted by Catalyst, the national nonprofit organization that works to foster the professional careers of women, indicates that these couples rate family even higher than careers in importance, and generally they have apparently always made decisions that benefit the family as a whole.

There are 25 million two-paycheck families and 4.7 million two-career families in the U.S. today. There is a difference between a two-paycheck family and two-career family. In a two-paycheck family, one or both spouses work primarily for the money. In a two-career family both partners are involved in lifelong commitments to work that involves personal growth and increasing responsibility. Some general characteristics of the two-paycheck family are:

- Commitment to employment to maintain family financial security
- The male as the primary wage earner

- The female in traditional house/child care role
- The female employment as "second" income
- Relocation issues determined by male wage earner options.

On the other hand, major trends observed in two-career families are usually:

- A major commitment to career progression
- Equal careers
- Both male and female as primary providers
- Family/parenting roles shared equally (however, not always proven to be so)
- Major decisions, including relocation, determined by mutual benefits to both partners.

Figure 8–1 outlines some of the major distinctions between the types of working couples.

FIGURE 8–1

TWO-PAYCHECK VERSUS TWO-CAREER FAMILIES

Major Issues	Two-Paycheck Family	Dual-Career Couples
Prime Goal	Pay bills/support family	Establish and maintain professional career
Commitment to Employment	Family financial security	Progression of careers
Primary types of jobs	Professional/Technical/Management Work/Career Commitment secondary to family/outside commitment	Professional/Technical/Management Primary commitment to both careers and family
Employment of spouse	Male-primary wage earner Female-secondary earner, work until married/pregnant	Male and female both considered primary providers
Family roles	Traditional family roles	Equal sharing of family roles based on choice/skills/time
Relocation	Determined by primary wage earner (usually male) limits options	Determined jointly to maximize both career opportunities, more options possible
Child care	Usually responsibility of female	Structured, well planned direction—both partners actively share responsibility

Both partners should recognize and acknowledge which of the two relationships they are in. Does your partner have the primary career and you the secondary career? Or is it the reverse? Is your arrangement one of alternating cycles of career development? Or are both careers of equal importance? Hence the necessity of maintaining both careers with as few sacrifices as possible personally and to the family life.

Although this chapter addresses families in which both spouses are employed, it may also help when unemployment has modified household roles. In a household in which only the husband once worked, the husband's unemployment may force the wife to go or return to work. Her working often causes role responsibilities to shift, with the male assuming the household management chores. The male may feel guilty about his wife's having to go to work, and the change in roles may even affect how he feels about himself. Alternatively, a newly unemployed male spouse has increased time at home, and he may assume many of the household responsibilities that his wife previously did. Conflict can arise if he doesn't cook the meals or wash the clothes the same way she does. Conflict may also arise if he doesn't assume any responsibility, even though he has more time. The wife may expect him to do some of "her" work.

EXERCISE 8–1: CLARIFYING ROLES/RESPONSIBILITIES

This exercise may help you and your partner clarify your roles/responsibilities as a working couple.

Instructions

You are to complete the fill-ins on the left. Your spouse is to complete those on the right.

I believe	*I believe*
____ We are a two-paycheck family.	____ We are a two-paycheck family.
____ We are a two-career couple.	____ We are a two-career couple.
____ My career is primary.	____ My career is primary.
____ My partner's career is primary.	____ My partner's career is primary.
____ Both careers are equally important.	____ Both careers are equally important.

I think my spouse believes:

_____ We are a two-paycheck family.

_____ We are a two-career couple.

_____ My career is primary.

_____ His/her career is primary.

_____ Both careers are equally important.

I think my spouse believes:

_____ We are a two-paycheck family.

_____ We are a two-career couple.

_____ My career is primary.

_____ His/her career is primary.

_____ Both careers are equally important.

Now complete the following statements:

1. Relationship issues that we concur on are:

- _____
- _____
- _____

2. Relationship issues that we disagree on are:

- _____
- _____
- _____

3. Issues to be resolved are: By Date:

- _____ _____
- _____ _____
- _____ _____

EXERCISE 8–2: STAGES OF RELATIONSHIP DEVELOPMENT

Working couples need to address other issues: not enough time, domestic responsibilities, child care, socialization, guilt, and money concerns. While these are common to all working couples, specific issues are prevalent in different age groups. Some of the major items that appear to surface frequently are listed in Figure 8–2.

These relationships are constantly changing, giving rise to always new problems. Your current solution may work for a period of time. If, however, something changes in your career, in your spouse's career, or in the family, you may find yourself considering another set of solutions. In most two-career family issues, the major constant seems to be change. The major coping methods entail accepting and adapting to change with a flexible, open attitude. Doing so requires effective, open communication between both partners and family members. If your career planning strategies are based on personal values and significantly different from your spouse's, you have to negotiate and reconcile the differences.

FIGURE 8–2
PROBLEMS IN RELATIONSHIP DEVELOPMENT

Couples in 20s

Long hours necessary to establish career
Decisions whether or not to have children
Delay in starting family
Providing child care
Quality and cost of child care
Professional rivalry
Job performance anxiety

Couples in 30s

Time demands
Guilt about "neglect" of partner/family
Need to have one partner with less stressful job to provide "emotional slack"
Pressures from families about having children
Medical concerns of further delaying pregnancy
Community/school obligations
Job relocation
Status rivalry with friends over buying home or possessions
Always feeling tired
Frustration of time limits
Increased financial obligations and pressures

Couples in 40s

Often female spouse entering/re-entering job market needs to spend all time/energy establishing career
Guilt over "neglect" of family
Family adjustment to new lifestyle, new roles
Partner in achievement stage and work time demands at premium
New set of household monetary rules—whose money is it? Who pays for what?
Feeling tired and pressured
Recognition of spouse as professional
Midlife crises, male/female

Couples in 50s

Often wife's career moving ahead, husband reaches top achievement state and ready to slow down and spend more time at home, with family, leisure activities
Changing structure of roles in family
Difficulty in relinquishing household responsibilities/chores
Time pressures
Spouse/partner illness, death, new financial responsibilities

FIGURE 8–2
(Cont.)

Couples in 60s

    Only one partner retired
    Pressures on other partner to retire
    Different interests
    Differing time schedules
    Family financial demands still pressing
    Reluctance to discuss retirement
    New/changing social relations

Student Families

    Putting spouse through school
    Child care/household responsibilities
    Partner/family "neglect"
    Generating long-term financial problems
    Delayed life/work satisfaction
    When schooling is early in marriage insufficient couple-bonding time

---

Instructions

Completing the following brief exercise may help to further clarify major issues for both partners. Place a check on the fill-in line next to the suitable option for either spouse, under Now or Future.

Husband		Wife		
Now	*Future*	*Now*	*Future*	*Career Planning Strategy*
——	——	——	——	*Take Turns:* Alternate whose career takes precedence.
——	——	——	——	*Two for the Road:* Both change jobs and relocate if both can find satisfactory jobs.
——	——	——	——	*For More Money, Power or Promise:* Change jobs if it means substantial increase in income, good promotion, or a promise of increased career opportunity.
——	——	——	——	*Time Out:* One partner takes time off while the other partner continues career such as to relocate overseas, go back to school, or have a child.
——	——	——	——	*Limited Geography:* Only specified geographical locations, usually major metropolitan areas, are considered to meet career and lifestyle needs.

RELOCATING THE TWO-CAREER FAMILY

Relocating is probably the most difficult problem facing dual-career couples. A survey of dual-career families strongly suggests that the career requirements of a spouse constitute the major reason for an employee's refusal to relocate . . .

Both of you are happy working at your respective organization. Suddenly you lose your job as a result of a merger or outplacement, and you find a new career opportunity 500 miles away. The new position could be a plus for your career, but disastrous for your spouse's career.

In such a situation, you and your partner face a set of difficult decisions. If you move, will your spouse (and family) relocate with you? If not, should you still move? If yes, what about your marriage? If not, what about your career? You have four basic options:

- Reject the offer
- Accept the offer, relocate the family, and spouse seeks new position
- Accept the position, relocate yourself, and commute on a regular basis
- Develop innovative solution acceptable to your spouse, his/her employer, and your family

To work through this complex issue, it is helpful to use a decision-making model that anticipates the outcomes and expectancies of each partner. Let's review some possible consequences of each of the four decisions.

Rejecting the offer

While a move may definitely improve your career potential, it may do nothing for your spouse who is currently very satisfied with his/her career and its potential. More and more couples are deciding against relocation for this reason. The move may increase the risk of losing one or both partner's professional identity. The quality of life at work and at home may also be jeopardized. Is the job really worth it? What are the possibilities for another opportunity if you refuse?

Accept the offer and relocate your family

Uprooting from a familiar work and community environment forces you to establish a new sense of belonging. One of the major consequences of relocation is a loss of personal, family, and professional identity. It takes time to build new personal and social relationships and to be accepted into a new organization and community. For many people this adjustment period, which can take up to one year, can be frustrating and depressing. The end of this transition can be identified by finally feeling more like an insider. Often your new position helps to create a new identity quickly, and it offers a sense of continuity during this transition adjustment. However, this may not be true for your spouse/family.

You probably feel you are in an "either/or" situation— "either" we stay together "or" our careers come first. Your spouse may have to make career sacrifices if he/she feels "forced" to relocate. He/she could possibly direct some anger toward your former employer. Such hostility may not surface immediately, but it could appear later as a personal/family crisis. As your unemployed partner waits for something to turn up, depression and resentment can be expected. If a satisfying job does not appear quickly, he/she may lose career identity and a sense of professional connectedness. Uprooted partners are more likely to experience considerable trauma if they have:

- A psychological involvement with the job to the extent that their self-concept is defined by work role
- An established career path and support network
- Few other life roles that are personally significant
- Never experienced job termination

Your partner is now experiencing the traumatic feelings you experienced as a result of your termination. Seriously evaluate these consequences before making a relocation decision. Determine the difference between what is desirable, what is appropriate, and what is manageable.

Accepting position and relocating yourself

If disruptions to your partner's career and family members are too involved to consider relocation, another option is to change your conventional living-together style, at least temporarily, and commute. This option is more feasible if your job requires considerable travel and time away from your family. It can be a realistic alternative if your partner has an established career, with little chance of relocation, or does not want to move.

If you are a highly career-oriented person, you may find that this lifestyle fits your career priorities by allowing you to totally immerse yourself into work while away from home. On weekends, you can concentrate on being with your spouse and family. If you experience role competition with your partner, generally this is significantly reduced.

Working/living apart is usually not motivated by economic reasons, but rather by personal and career-growth reasons. *Business Week* reported in 1978 that commuting couples can spend over $10,000 (1978 dollars) in travel alone. Phone calls increase these costs significantly, plus the cost for reliable child-care and home management assistance. Obviously, then, you both must have salaries that can support this lifestyle.

You also have to consider the emotional costs of separation. Constant planning is necessary to assure maximum benefits of your time together. Communication is intensified, and you may have little time for outside socializing. Loneliness becomes a major factor. Trust in each other is essential. Researchers on commuting couples agree that the biggest factor in making a commuting lifestyle work is the strength of your relationship. Both partners must be committed to this arrangement and share a strong trust in one another.

You therefore need to ask yourself if you can sustain your identity and relationships as a couple and as a family without living together all the time. Will the opportunity to develop your professional career strengthen or threaten your marriage/family life? Harvard Business School research has found that commuting arrangements are difficult to handle, and few couples survive them.

Commuters' arrangements generally work best when:

1. Work arrangements permit job scheduling flexibility—that is, if the commuting partner can schedule days off, work at home occasionally, leave early, and arrive late to accommodate travel schedules.
2. You work out travel logistics and plan to be together on a regular basis.
3. You take vacations together.
4. Maintain frequent telephone contact. (You might make sure that you can use your employer's toll free number.)
5. You should plan to get together at least once a month and more often if possible. If you have younger children, you may want to spend every weekend together. Generally, the commuting lifestyle works best when children are at least high school age.
6. There are general ground rules regarding social contacts, parties, dating. Avoiding the issue is likely to lead to trouble. It's best to take the time and define these ground rules in advance, agreeing not to alter them without prior consultation.

Be sure to spend time discussing responsibilities for the partner who is staying at home. Who will fill in for the partner on the road? Regardless of whether mom or dad is there, dishwashers break down, cars overheat, and children still get the measles. Standby help should be lined up for such emergencies. If you decide on commuting, view this option as experimental before completely rearranging your present lifestyle.

Develop innovative solutions

If you develop your own solutions, you most likely have to bargain with your prospective employer as well as with your spouse.

- Living apart on a temporary basis is one possibility. Try out the new location and have time for your spouse to look for a new job without giving up her/his position.

- Assuming you and your spouse share similar backgrounds, consider seeking a "job-sharing" position—both you and your spouse for the price of one.
- Your spouse may request a leave of absence with a "guaranteed right to return." If this is granted, be certain to ask for and obtain the guarantee in writing, specifying that the same or an equivalent position will be available on return. Make sure the guarantee is not qualified with any conditions like "if there is a position available." Management may be persuaded to agree to these conditions.

EXERCISE 8–3: WHICH OPTION WILL WE TAKE?

Instructions

This exercise can help clarify your thinking about your options. Assign a risk factor (Low, Med, or High) to the likelihood of each outcome, or consequence. (The Relocation Worksheets from Chapter 6 are also very helpful in generating additional consequences for your four alternatives.) Then formulate a tentative decision and a date for making a final decision.

Option 1
REJECTING THE OFFER

	Consequences	Low	Med	High
1.				
2.				
3.				
4.				
5.				
6.				
7.				
8.				
9.				
10.				

Risks

Option II
ACCEPTING OFFER AND RELOCATION OF FAMILY

Consequences	Risks		
	Low	Med	High
1. _____	____	____	____
2. _____	____	____	____
3. _____	____	____	____
4. _____	____	____	____
5. _____	____	____	____
6. _____	____	____	____
7. _____	____	____	____
8. _____	____	____	____
9. _____	____	____	____
10. _____	____	____	____

Option III
ACCEPTING POSITION AND COMMUTING

Consequences	Risks		
	Low	Med	High
1. _____	____	____	____
2. _____	____	____	____
3. _____	____	____	____
4. _____	____	____	____
5. _____	____	____	____
6. _____	____	____	____
7. _____	____	____	____
8. _____	____	____	____
9. _____	____	____	____
10. _____	____	____	____

Option IV
DEVELOPING AN INNOVATIVE, ACCEPTABLE SOLUTION

	Consequences	Risks		
		Low	Med	High
1.	_____	____	____	____
2.	_____	____	____	____
3.	_____	____	____	____
4.	_____	____	____	____
5.	_____	____	____	____
6.	_____	____	____	____
7.	_____	____	____	____
8.	_____	____	____	____
9.	_____	____	____	____
10.	_____	____	____	____

Our tentative decision is _____

_____

_____

_____

Date to make final decision: _____

NEW WAYS OF HELPING DUAL-CAREER COUPLES

Responsive corporations are currently helping dual-career couples in a variety of ways.

If a company holds membership in the Employment Management Association (EMA), they can provide a sophisticated corporate support network for your spouse in facilitating his/her job hunting campaign. This service, instituted early 1981, works as follows: An employer-member of EMA contacts the association to request services for a particular situation. For example, you may be relocating from New York to Chicago with your new company, and your spouse, a marketing manager for a large manufacturer, will be looking for a position. EMA sends a list of corporations and contact names

(EMA members and corporations on their general mailing list) in the Chicago area to your spouse. EMA also sends a set of cards, one of which, when attached to your spouse's resume, flags it as part of the EMA relocation assistance program.

The program eases your spouse's entry into an unfamiliar job market by eliminating the tedious search for contacts. It also develops a sense of "top priority" for your spouse's flagged resume and provides quick attention that is so critical for relocating families.

If you are relocating to the Northern New Jersey/ Connecticut area, a job information bank, focusing on managerial and professional jobs, is available for individuals with well-defined, established careers who are looking for specific job information. The program was developed jointly by Home Buyer's Assistance Corporation (HBAC), Merck & Company, Inc., and Rutgers University. To use the system, your organization requests HBAC to assist your relocating spouse. HBAC reviews the individual's experience and job objective, and then it matches this objective with information in the job bank. The job bank information is based on a detailed survey of the jobs for which each corporation often recruits. Your spouse is given a list of corporations with appropriate job descriptions and the names of contacts. The list does *not* represent actual job openings. In the future, HBAC hopes to expand the system to service New York City.

More and more companies are also offering unstructured job assistance to relocated spouses. Ask for it.

WHO DOES HOUSEHOLD MANAGEMENT TASKS?

In a two-career home, the power between partners tends to be equally distributed. Household management tasks need to be done but at a personal cost to both. It seems only "fair" for partners to share the burden of managing a home. Both partners bargain for what they will, won't, can, or cannot do. Two-career couples must recognize the need to change their expectations about who does what at home. Any change in family structure—such as when one partner is unemployed, begins a new position, or relocates—new job demands may give rise to another set of time demands. Thus a discussion of "who does what" and an opportunity to renegotiate activities may be in order.

Instructions

The Planning/Discussion worksheets in Figures 8–2 and 8–3 provide a method for planning, discussing, and negotiating the couple's division of labor. In Figure 8–2, you should check the appropriate column if the husband does the task, if the wife does the task, if both do it, or if neither do it (that is, hired help does it.) Have your spouse do the same for Figure 8–3. Each of you should complete the separate sheets prior to the discussion to clarify individual expectations. The resulting plan should be limited to a specific stated period of time and then reassessed and revised, again for a specific time period.

FIGURE 8–2:

DIVISION OF LABOR ON HOUSEHOLD MANAGEMENT TASKS [SELF]

Time period: Beginning _____ Ending _____

	Who Does It Now?				Who Will Do It?			
	Husband	Wife	Both	Neither/ Other	Husband	Wife	Both	Neither/ Other
Food chores:								
Shopping	—	—	—	—	—	—	—	—
Cooking	—	—	—	—	—	—	—	—
Kitchen cleanup	—	—	—	—	—	—	—	—
Garbage	—	—	—	—	—	—	—	—
Packing Lunches	—	—	—	—	—	—	—	—
Clothes chores:								
Shopping	—	—	—	—	—	—	—	—
Washing	—	—	—	—	—	—	—	—
Folding	—	—	—	—	—	—	—	—
Putting away	—	—	—	—	—	—	—	—
Dry cleaning	—	—	—	—	—	—	—	—
Mending	—	—	—	—	—	—	—	—
Ironing	—	—	—	—	—	—	—	—
Weeding out old clothes	—	—	—	—	—	—	—	—

FIGURE 8-2
(Cont.)

	Who Does It Now?				Who Will Do It?			
	Husband	Wife	Both	Neither/ Other	Husband	Wife	Both	Neither/ Other
Money chores:								
Budget planning	___	___	___	___	___	___	___	___
Bill paying	___	___	___	___	___	___	___	___
Bank accounts	___	___	___	___	___	___	___	___
House/apartment maintenance:								
Cleaning	___	___	___	___	___	___	___	___
Appliance maintenance	___	___	___	___	___	___	___	___
Lawn or yard	___	___	___	___	___	___	___	___
Furnace	___	___	___	___	___	___	___	___
Storms, screens, etc.	___	___	___	___	___	___	___	___
House repairs	___	___	___	___	___	___	___	___
Dealing with service people	___	___	___	___	___	___	___	___
Social Obligations:								
Gift buying	___	___	___	___	___	___	___	___
Entertaining	___	___	___	___	___	___	___	___
Holiday/birthday obligations	___	___	___	___	___	___	___	___
Coordinating family's social schedules	___	___	___	___	___	___	___	___
Children:								
School meetings	___	___	___	___	___	___	___	___
Driving	___	___	___	___	___	___	___	___
Support for activities/scouts, etc.	___	___	___	___	___	___	___	___

FIGURE 8–2
(Cont.)

	Who Does It Now?				Who Will Do It?			
	Husband	Wife	Both	Neither/ Other	Husband	Wife	Both	Neither/ Other
Volunteer work on children's activities	——	——	——	——	——	——	——	——
Pets:								
Daily care	——	——	——	——	——	——	——	——
Regular maintenance (Vet)	——	——	——	——	——	——	——	——
Boarding for Vacations	——	——	——	——	——	——	——	——
Leisure:								
Planning social activities	——	——	——	——	——	——	——	——
Vacation arrangements	——	——	——	——	——	——	——	——
Weekend activities	——	——	——	——	——	——	——	——
Other tasks unique to your household:								
	——	——	——	——	——	——	——	——
	——	——	——	——	——	——	——	——
	——	——	——	——	——	——	——	——
	——	——	——	——	——	——	——	——
	——	——	——	——	——	——	——	——
	——	——	——	——	——	——	——	——
	——	——	——	——	——	——	——	——
	——	——	——	——	——	——	——	——
	——	——	——	——	——	——	——	——

FIGURE 8–3

DIVISION OF LABOR ON HOUSEHOLD MANAGEMENT TASKS [SPOUSE]

Time Period: Beginning _____ Ending _____

| | Who Does It Now? | | | | Who Will Do It? | | | |
	Husband	Wife	Both	Neither/ Other	Husband	Wife	Both	Neither/ Other
Food Chores:								
Shopping	___	___	___	___	___	___	___	___
Cooking	___	___	___	___	___	___	___	___
Kitchen cleanup	___	___	___	___	___	___	___	___
Garbage	___	___	___	___	___	___	___	___
Packing lunches	___	___	___	___	___	___	___	___
Clothes Chores:								
Shopping	___	___	___	___	___	___	___	___
Washing	___	___	___	___	___	___	___	___
Folding	___	___	___	___	___	___	___	___
Putting away	___	___	___	___	___	___	___	___
Dry cleaning	___	___	___	___	___	___	___	___
Mending	___	___	___	___	___	___	___	___
Ironing	___	___	___	___	___	___	___	___
Weeding out old clothes	___	___	___	___	___	___	___	___
Money Chores:								
Budget planning	___	___	___	___	___	___	___	___
Bill paying	___	___	___	___	___	___	___	___
Bank accounts	___	___	___	___	___	___	___	___
House/apartment maintenance:								
Cleaning	___	___	___	___	___	___	___	___
Appliance maintenance	___	___	___	___	___	___	___	___
Lawn or yard	___	___	___	___	___	___	___	___
Furnace	___	___	___	___	___	___	___	___
Storms, screens, etc.	___	___	___	___	___	___	___	___

FIGURE 8–3
(Cont.)

	Who Does It Now?				Who Will Do It?			
	Husband	Wife	Both	Neither/Other	Husband	Wife	Both	Neither Other
House repairs	___	___	___	___	___	___	___	___
Dealing with service people	___	___	___	___	___	___	___	___
Social obligations:								
Gift buying	___	___	___	___	___	___	___	___
Entertaining	___	___	___	___	___	___	___	___
Holiday/birthday obligations	___	___	___	___	___	___	___	___
Coordinating family's social schedules	___	___	___	___	___	___	___	___
Children:								
School meetings	___	___	___	___	___	___	___	___
Driving	___	___	___	___	___	___	___	___
Support for Activities/scouts, etc.	___	___	___	___	___	___	___	___
Volunteer work on children's activities	___	___	___	___	___	___	___	___
Pets:								
Daily care	___	___	___	___	___	___	___	___
Regular maintenance (Vet)	___	___	___	___	___	___	___	___
Boarding for vacations	___	___	___	___	___	___	___	___
Leisure:								
Planning social activities	___	___	___	___	___	___	___	___
Vacation arrangements	___	___	___	___	___	___	___	___
Weekend activities	___	___	___	___	___	___	___	___

Many of us may not enjoy doing some household management tasks. We may experience ambivalence, guilt, jealousy, or resentment about switching roles. Talking through our feelings about roles is important, since role sharing may often involve the loss of ego satisfaction. It may be difficult for a wife to admit that her husband is a better cook than she, or for a husband to say that his wife's handier around the house than he is. Both are experiencing a loss of ego identity developed through previous sex role expectations.

Instructions

Partners should individually complete the following sections before discussing their reactions.

For completion by you

1. What feelings do I have about my role-sharing arrangements?

   _____

   _____

   _____

   _____

2. How do I feel about giving up my "territory"?

   _____

   _____

   _____

   _____

   _____

3. How trusting am I of my partner to perform these tasks? How willing am I to allow him/her to make mistakes or to do things differently?

_____

_____

_____

_____

4. How do I feel about "going public"—that is, letting others know that things are different at home?

_____

_____

_____

_____

For completion by partner

1. What feelings do I have about my role-sharing arrangements?

_____

_____

_____

_____

2. How do I feel about giving up my "territory"?

_____

_____

_____

_____

3. How trusting am I of my partner to perform these tasks? How willing am I to allow him/her to make mistakes or to do things differently?

_____

_____

_____

_____

_____

4. How do I feel about "going public"—that is, letting others know that things are different at home?

_____

_____

_____

_____

_____

References for Further Reading

Bird, Caroline. *The Two Paycheck Family*. New York: Rawson, Wade Publications, 1979.

Catalyst National Survey Report. *Two-Career Families and Their Employers*. New York: Catalyst, 1981.

Hall, Francine, S., and Douglas T. Hall. *The Two-Career Couple*. Reading, Mass.: Addison-Wesley Publishing Company, 1979.

Shaevitz, Marjorie Hansen, and Morton H. Shaevitz. *Making it Together*. Boston, Mass.: Houghton-Mifflin Company, 1980.

9

Developing your marketing strategies

You have something to sell. You are selling your time, your experience, your education, your potential. To do so effectively, you need a marketing plan, just as you would for any salable product. Thus you need tools for use in your sales campaign:

- a resume,
- a contact network, and
- letters.

RESUME

One of the major tools in today's employment process is a resume. A resume does not get you a job, but a well designed and thought-out resume serves as an introduction. It gets you an interview, and interviews get jobs.

An effective resume packages you well. It is an advertisement for you. It is neither an autobiography, nor an application form, but rather a compilation of selected facts organized to create impressions that you want to make on the interviewer. It quickly and clearly tells the person that you are qualified for the position you are seeking. Most employers are looking for specific people to fill specific jobs. They want people who can solve problems. If you have worked through the material in Chapters 3–5, you now know what you want to do, what problems you can solve, and what you have to offer. In that case, the following worksheets help you get started on the first draft of your resume.

Throughout the process of creating your resume, remember:

- Emphasize your important assets.
- Each statement should be accurate, neither exaggerated nor underplayed.
- Write as if you were writing a telegram; avoid the personal pronoun.
- Everything on your resume should sell you.
- Resumes basically need to be succinct, easy to read, and graphically open.

Your resume is a unique, dynamic factual presentation of you at your best. It should also be an indication of *future* achievements. An employer can only hire your future. A resume should therefore do the following:

- present your job and career objectives in terms of your assets;
- prove that your job objective is realistic and documented by your accomplishments;
- put you in control of the interview by stating what you want to talk about to the interviewer.

EXERCISE 9–1: FIRST DRAFT

The purpose of the first draft is to build a "case" for yourself. At this point, the final format of the resume is not important. Write your first draft in pencil. Make only factual statements since you must prove what you say. Provide pertinent information to help the interviewer understand what you want to do and what your qualifications are for carrying out your intentions.

Identification

Your name, address, and telephone number should go on the top of your resume. Do not include other data, such as height, weight, or Social Security number. Include a business telephone number and extension, only if being contacted at that number is not a problem for you. Do not abbreviate.

Name _____

Address _____

City _____ State _____ Zip _____

Phone [Home]   (Area Code)   _____

    [Office]   (Area Code)   _____

Objective

The objective is the most important of your resume. It is a statement of purpose that must gain the interviewer's immediate attention. The rest of the resume must document this objective. Using the information from the Career Analysis Summary in Exercise 5–9, state your objective in clear and concise language. Write your job objective to include your major skill areas. Express your objective in terms of job functions rather than job titles. It should also include specific results that you could produce for an employer.

Professional Objective: _____

_____

_____

_____

_____

Qualifications

This section of the resume is a concise summary of the major areas of experience that support your objective. It can be written in narrative style, or in single-word, outline form, but it must be brief, clear, and easy to scan.

Summary of Qualifications _____

_____

_____

_____

_____

_____

Education

List your highest degree first, with lesser degrees following. List your high school diploma if you do not have post-secondary degrees. Add continuing education and training if it is relevant to your objective. List any academic, technical, or state certifications.

If your major does not strongly support your objective, drop the major and list only the degree and the university.

If you are about to receive a degree in the near future, indicate the degree and when you will receive it with the word "candidate" inserted after the degree.

If you have advanced degrees that may "overqualify" you for the position you are seeking, you may wish to exclude the degrees and put "Graduate work in . . . at . . ."

If your education relates directly to your objectives, list it immediately after your objective. If it does not immediately support your stated objective, list it near the end of your resume.

Education: _____

_____

_____

_____

_____

_____

_____

Achievements

Select the two strongest, specific examples in support of each of the areas of strengths listed in your objective and qualifications statement. Be sure the words and phrases you use relate clearly to your objective. Use language that the reader/interviewer can easily understand. Begin each achievement with action verbs, such as "sold" "persuaded" "implemented" "organized" "created." You may wish to capitalize or underscore these verbs so they stand out. Refer to Exercise 4–3 on p. 56 for your motivated skills.

This section could be headlined by one of the following:

- Professional Accom-
  plishments
- Demonstrated Results
- Examples of Effectiveness
- Indications of Potential
- Related Accomplishments
- Results
- Career-Related
  Achievements

Six to ten examples could be listed and prioritized to support your objective:

- _____
  _____

- _____
  _____
  _____

- _____
  _____

- _____
  _____

- _____
  _____

- _____
  _____
  _____
- _____
  _____
  _____
- _____
  _____
  _____
- _____
  _____
  _____
- _____
  _____
  _____
- _____
  _____
  _____
- _____
  _____
  _____

Work experience/employment history

Using the Career Progression Assessment Tool (Figure 4–6) on pages 60–61 as a guide, start with the most recent, or most relevant position, and list your job title, your employer, city, and a brief description of your major job functions. Put the dates of employment (years only) at the end of this statement. Avoid listing dates on the left or right margin where they become the center of attention. It is better to have the interviewer's attention on *what* you did rather than *when* you did it.

If your former job titles do not accurately reflect your responsibilities, use function titles that the interviewer will understand.

In describing your duties, emphasize the ones that relate directly to your objective.

If the employment dates appear to give negative information about you, leave them out. However, you should always try to show continuous employment. Unpaid work should be listed if it supports the objective.

Work Experience: First Entry

_____

_____

_____

Second Entry

_____

_____

_____

Third Entry

_____

_____

_____

_____

Fourth Entry

_____

_____

_____

_____

Fifth Entry

_____

_____

_____

_____

Other supportive data

List relevant memberships, awards, publications, and patents if they support your objectives. In some cases, personal interests relate to the objective and therefore should be listed. If you have foreign language ability, list it if it supports the objective.

Professional Memberships: _____

_____

_____

Awards: _____

_____

_____

Publications: _____

_____

_____

Patents: _____

_____

_____

Personal

List only the following personal data: health, marital status, children. Of that, list only what is an asset to you. Make certain that the information you give cannot be interpreted negatively. You will be in a more favorable position during the interview to add more information if requested.

Personal: _____

_____

_____

_____

_____

References

Never include references on a resume, and they are not offered until requested by a potential employer. Three to five references are usually enough, but they should be individuals who are able to evaluate your work as well as your personal characteristics. Be sure to personally contact your references before giving their names to prospective employers. What they say about you can sometimes be a decisive factor in a job offer. So be sure they are well informed about your job campaign and the type of position you are seeking.

Have the reference's names, titles, organizations, addresses, and telephone numbers typed and well organized to present to an interviewer when you are asked for them.

SECOND DRAFT

Recheck all information in your resume to make sure it supports your objective. Trim all unnecessary words. It should be one page, with a maximum of two pages.

Decide on the format you would like to use. See Figures 9–1 through 9–7.

Arrange major headings in order of importance, try various layouts, and determine which has the best appearance and impact for you.

Make use of spacing, capital letters, and underscoring to direct the interviewer's attention to the strongest and most important elements of your resume.

YOUR FINAL, FINISHED RESUME

Your resume is part of your total presentation, verbal as well as visual. Your final resume should be printed on a good rag bond paper. White paper is preferred, but light shades are acceptable. Do not mimeograph it.

FIGURE 9–1 SAMPLE

NAME
14726 Park Avenue
Gig Harbor, Washington 98335
206–928-3591
206–331-2800

PROFESSIONAL OBJECTIVE:

MANAGER, ENGINEERING or other responsible STAFF ENGINEERING POSITION utilizing my skills and extensive experience in design, planning, systems developments, and supervision.

SUMMARY OF QUALIFICATIONS:

- Design Department Supervisor—8 years
- Mechanical Project Engineer/Manager—7 years
- Related Design Engineering Work—7 years

CAREER EXPERIENCE: Harris Engineering, Tacoma, Washington

Senior Project Engineer/Manager
Manage, control and execute plant facilities and chemical process projects. Formulate and implement engineering programs for chemical plant process system improvement.
Derive project conceptions, definition analysis, estimates, appropriation request preparation, material specifications, design and drafting.
Contract administration and follow-up construction; operating instructions and system start-ups.
Responsible for project monies, construction schedules.
Consistently meeting target dates and operating under budget costs.

Supervisor/Project Manager, Design Department
Individually developed and broadened growth of design team from a 5 to 18 man efficient and economic Design Engineering Department. Sparked motivation and upgraded individual designer's productivity from 2.20 to 3.30 mechanical piping design drawings per man month. Responsible for providing all disciplines of engineering design services for Tacoma and out of state plant sites.
Interviewed, hired or terminated personnel as required. Evaluated staff performances. Administered rewards and disciplines; established and accomplished goals. (1972–1982)

Senior Design Engineer
Prepared complete design engineering packages and specifications for major projects. Developed innovative designs for diaphragm cell (patent applied for) Special merit recognition from Research.

FIGURE 9–1
(Cont.)

Also special merit recognition, Engineering, for liquification system design. (1968–1972)

CAREER EXPERIENCE: Aramco, Republic of S. Vietnam

Mechanical Engineer
Board and field construction work, initiating design completions and improvements.
Requisitioned materials and initiated field construction and followed up completion of air conditioning systems totalling 1,835 tons; also supervised 4,000 kw electrical power generation stations, and water well drilling programs with installation of 20 miles of related water piping distribution systems.
Responsible for all reporting, liaison, correspondence, trouble-shooting, start-up, inspection and aerodynamic balance of air conditioning systems.
Completed work under enemy harrassment and constant physical and mental hardships at remote U.S. Army outposts through South Vietnam. Company was awarded the "U.S. Navy Certificate of Merit Award" for its achievements, and received awards from the President of the Republic of South Vietnam. (1966–1968)

EDUCATION:

B.S. Mechanical Engineering
University of Washington

Drafting Diploma
Indiana Institute of Technology

PROFESSIONAL AFFILIATIONS:

Professional Mechanical Engineer license—Washington, Indiana
Engineering Society of Seattle/Tacoma
American Society of Mechanical Engineers

FIGURE 9–2 Sample

NAME
27252 Bonn
Dearborn Heights, Michigan 48127
313–651–7161

Objective: *Supervisor:* whereby my experience in leadership, accomplishment of goals and innovations of practical systems could reduce costs while maintaining efficiency.

Qualifications: Assistant manager of railroad unloading
Customer service
Supervised receiving dock operations
Head order selector of stationery line operations

Achievements: *Supervised* railroad unloading dock during extended absence of supervisor

Motivated three-man crew to set record by unloading six box cars within eight-hour period

Reduced inventory by collecting and organizing old stock to be shipped back to the manufacturer for credit, eliminating unwanted merchandise while reducing cost and providing room for better selling items

Organized stockroom for airplane engine and structure parts and accessories, increasing mechanics efficiency

Experience: *Order-Selector:* Lewis Paper Company, Detroit, Michigan (1977–present)
Handle rush orders and customer pick-up orders
Filling in at head of line operation

Box Car Unloader: Lewis Paper Company, Detroit, Michigan (1974–1977)
Handling power equipment in unloading of box cars
Assisted in management of box car operations

Band-saw Operator: Fort Wayne Manufacturing Company, Fort Wayne, Indiana (1973–1974)
Learned to make various parts and cuts with little supervision. Shop maintenance.

FIGURE 9–2
(CONT.)

> *Maintenance Worker:* Harrisburg—Raleigh Airport,
> Raleigh, Illinois (1968–1972)
> Light work on aircraft
> Refueling operations
> Organized and managed stockroom

Education: Philosophy/Psychology   3 years
Drafting Technology   1 year

Personal: 23
Married
One child
Excellent health

FIGURE 9–3 SAMPLE

NAME
28252 Jane
Plymouth, Michigan 48170
313/456–3891

Objective: *Financial Management* in which experience and training are utilized in an administrative, decision-making capacity.

Background: *Summary:* Management experience includes analysis, planning and forecasting of corporate accounts; the evaluation, structuring and negotiation of corporate loans; development of customer relations: personnel training and supervision.
Education: MBA (Finance) Wayne State University
BBA (Finance) Wayne State University

Selected *Management:*
Accomplishments: Currently managing $12 million loan portfolio of 150 accounts.
Increased loan portfolio by $10 million in two years.
Prevented a $200,000 bank loss by working with client's attorneys and bankruptcy court to restructure and renegotiate loan.

FIGURE 9–3
(CONT.)

Communications:
Negotiation of loan agreements with corporate and individual clients.

As a member of a loan committee, presented financial analysis and evaluated profitability of loans.

Improved customer relations through effective communication and the development of rapport and confidence.

Training and Supervision: Train and supervise financial analysts.

Employment History:

Manufacturers National Bank
Detroit, Michigan (1975–Present)

Assistant Vice President: Responsible for corporate loan and account management for clients of up to $20 million sales volume, including service organizations, retailers, wholesalers, real estate developers, and manufacturers.

Direct the financial analysis, forecasting and loan negotiations relating to the portfolio.

Credit Analyst: Handled financial analysis of companies ranging in size from small, local firms to billion dollar multinational corporations. Work group leader supervising four analysts.

Other experience while attending college includes merchandising management, investment analysis and contribution to the writing and editing of a textbook.

Personal:

Bonded   Excellent Health   Married

FIGURE 9–4 SAMPLE

NAME
1246 Page Lane
Ann Arbor, Michigan 48104
313–427—6129

Job Objective:

A responsible *clerical* position, utilizing my skills in public and human relations, organization, management and secretarial experiences.

SUMMARY OF QUALIFICATIONS:

- Management and Supervision
- Inventory Control
- Payroll
- Computer Terminal Operator
- Office Machines, Typing [70 wpm]
- Office Procedures, Shorthand [50 wpm]
- Insurance Billings
- Accounts Receivables

EMPLOYMENT EXPERIENCE:

Salesperson. Self-employed. 1981–present.
Scheduled appointments and meetings with prospective customers.
Public speaking.

Computer Terminal Operator. General Motors Truck & Coach Division, Pontiac, Michigan 1980–1981
Operated computer terminals and read blue-prints for repaired parts.

Quality Control Inspector & Assembler. Pontiac Motors, Pontiac, Michigan 1979–1980.

Office Clerk. Wayne County Community College. Detroit, Michigan 1978
Performed general office activities which included: typing, filing, answering phones and providing general information.

Assistant Manager/Bookkeeper. Skateland, Inc. Grosse Pointe, Michigan 1976–1978
Public Relations, Accounts Receivables, Coordinated sales.

Receptionist. Keith Underwriters, Inc. Pontiac, Michigan 1974–1976
Insurance billings, filing, customer relations, typed claims and application forms, general shorthand.

File Clerk & Secretarial Pool. Medical Auxilliary, Birmingham, Michigan 1973

EDUCATION:

Business courses in Typing, Speedwriting, Dictation, and English at Pontiac Opportunity Industrial Center

Course in Career Assessment and Planning, Oakland University, Summer, 1982

Diploma, Pontiac Central High School

PERSONAL:

Single, Head of Household, Excellent Health

FIGURE 9–5 SAMPLE

NAME
970 Park Drive
Detroit, Michigan 48201
313–891–6307
(Messages)   313–249–9595

JOB OBJECTIVES:

Machinist position, leading to a Robotics Technician, using my background in operating industrial machines in precision technology.

SUMMARY OF QUALIFICATIONS:

Fifteen years of Machinist-related experience includes:

- Blue Print Drafting
- OD/ID Grinders
- Lathes
- Mills
- Hydraulics
- Pneumatic & Compressors
- Die Setting
- Plumbing
- Sheet Metal Mechanic
- Industrial Painting

EDUCATION:

Courses in Machine Shop, Schoolcraft College, 1970

Currently enrolled in the Robotics Training Program, Oakland Community College

Diploma, Bentley High School, Livonia. Courses in Blue Print reading and co-op student in welding program

RESULTS:

- Set up and operated Grinders OD/ID within .001, using blue prints and precision gauges.
- As a sheet metal mechanic, set up prototype parts before production began.
- Refitted boilers and heating systems with valves.
- Experienced as an electrician in wiring, soldering and welding; Electrical mechanic in repairing and cleaning motors.

EMPLOYMENT HISTORY:

Spray Painter. General Motors Truck and Coach Division, Pontiac, Michigan   1981–1982

Grinder & Mechanic. 1978–1981.
Did blueprint reading, set up Grinders OD/ID and precision gauges.

Electrician, Plumber & Mechanic. Waterford School, Waterford, Michigan
Welded and soldered; cleaned and refitted boilers; installed shut-off valves in heating system; wired lights and plugs; operated trucks, tractors, and front-end loader.   1975–1978

Machinist. Lattimore & Tessemer, Livonia, Michigan

FIGURE 9–5
(Cont.)

Operated surface grinders, mills, band saw, sander, lathe;
Used hand tools and drill press; Did blue print reading; Worked with Precision
Gauges—micrometers; calipers; dial indicators; snap gauges.   1971–1974

Grinder and Mill Operator. Yale Die Sinking and Engraving, Livonia, Michigan   1970–1971

Die Setter. Nemco, Novi, Michigan
Set dies and operated large presses.   1969–1970

Welder & Press Operator. Paragon Steel Company, Novi, Michigan
Used cutting torches, hot riveters, welding and drill press.   1965–1968

PERSONAL:
Married, 4 Children   Excellent Health

FIGURE 9–6 Sample

NAME
433 Jones Street
Springfield, Vermont 05403
802–259–9935   Ext. 4159 (Work)
802–671–9118   (Residence)

POSITION SOUGHT:

A position in GENERAL PLANT MAINTENANCE.

SUMMARY OF QUALIFICATIONS:

Five years of mechanical experience includes:

Equipment Repair and Maintenance	Carpentry and Woodwork
Equipment Installation	Auto and Diesel Mechanic
Welding and Fabrication	Roofing and Painting
Basic Electrical	Licensed Boiler Operator
Pipefitting	Licensed Hi-Lo Driver

WORK HISTORY:

Various responsibilities at Scott Chemical Works, Springfield, Vermont include:

Sample Room Attendant (1982–1983)
Collected pigment samples for industrial customer requests. Labeled and packaged products for shipping.

Plant Maintenance Worker (1982)
Installed and repaired plant equipment. Did welding, pipefitting, electrical, plumbing, carpentry, roofing, glazing, masonry and lathe work. Maintained diesels and worked on boilers under experienced supervisor.

Welder, Mac's Welding Company, Central City, Vermont (1981–1982) Set up and operated shape cutter; cut, torched materials, bending and shearing for welding; fabrication of finished products.

Linecutter and Welder, Smith Steel and Welding, Central City, Vermont (1977–1981)
Did cutting; operated shapecutter, shearing, bending and sawing, completed customer work orders.

EDUCATION:

Diploma, Springfield High School, 1978.
Course in "Steam Boiler Operator" N.A.P.E., Central City Community Education

PERSONAL:

Single, excellent health

FIGURE 9–7 Sample

NAME
44 North Main
Austin, Texas 78711
542–781–0597   (Residence)

POSITION SOUGHT:

Laboratory Research Technician, using my analytical and research skills.

Summary of Qualifications:

Two years of technical experience includes:

Research Methods	Logging and Record Keeping of Samples
Analytical Procedures	Instrumental Analysis

CAREER HISTORY:

Increasing responsibilities at F. Frank Chemical Corporation, Dallas, Texas include:

Laboratory Technician (1981–Present)
Assisted chemists in conducting experiments, made observations, recorded data and reported results. Operated analytical equipment to test samples. Tested printing inks in nitrocellulose, waterflexo and pallimide. Read draw-downs for proper printing properties. Tested presscake of pigment in wet form.

Utility Worker (1979–1981)
Maintained all solvents. Organized an RX system. Recorded location of samples. Provided equipment for chemists when needed. Delivered UPS packages within plant site.

Hostess/Cook McDonald's Corporation, Dallas, Texas (1979)

EDUCATION:

High School Diploma, First Christian School, Benson, Texas.
Course in Assertiveness Training, in-house program, F. Frank Chemical Corporation.

PERSONAL:

Married, Excellent Health

DEVELOPING MARKETING LEADS AND CONTACTS

How did you find your family doctor? Your lawyer? The best mechanic in town? You probably will get your best job leads the same way—by asking people! Developing job leads takes time and patience, but it produces results.

One particularly productive approach is to spend two or three full days researching, copying, and collating information from the sources listed below. Most of these sources are in your local library, and library staff persons are very helpful.

- Dun and Bradstreet, *Million Dollar and Middle Market Directory*
- Standard and Poor's *Register of Corporations, Directors, and Executives*, Volumes I, II, III
- *Thomas's Register of American Manufacturers*
- *Moody's Manuals*
- Harris State Industrial Directories

The following list may also be helpful in identifying further leads:

- Trade publications
- Civic organizations
- Professional organizations
- Chamber of commerce
- Forty-Plus Club
- The Yellow Pages
- Company annual reports
- College placement/alumni listings
- Newsletters
- Trustees/board of directors (usually can arrange interviews)
- Executive search firms
- Employment agencies
- Newspaper ads (local, *Wall Street Journal*)
- Job shops
- Direct mail campaigns

Any and/or all of these sources can be helpful. They are certainly worth a try, and you can determine their merits for yourself. Don't waste your time on any source that does not fit your needs.

Check out employment agencies carefully. As in any business, there are some very good ones and some that are not so good. Use only the services with established reputations. Basically there are two types of agency agreements: In one, the employer pays the fee; in the other, you, the applicant, are responsible for payment to the agency. A word of caution: Read *any* contract very carefully—including the fine print. Often, there may be clauses relating to specific circumstances that would hold you financially responsible for fee payments. State immediately that you are only interested in fee-paid jobs. Do *not* sign anything. If you find a service you are comfortable working with, keep in touch, keep them informed of your activities, and keep after them to see what they are doing for you.

Executive search firms operate differently. They are hired by an organization to identify candidates to fill a specific, existing job vacancy. While it is always flattering to be contacted by a "head hunter," remember that they are doing the selling. So listen carefully and ask a lot of questions. Search firms usually recruit from the ranks of the employed and in the $30,000-plus range.

EXERCISE 9–2: PERSONAL CONTACT WORK

Your contact list should consist of people who would recognize your name if you sent them a letter. They do not have to be good friends. You may want to start by examining your personal telephone/mailing list. Brainstorm the following areas with a spouse/friend, and jot down as many names as you can think of. At this point, do not evaluate whether you will contact them.

Who do you know that is a . . .

Former Employer	Lawyers
Bankers (local branch managers)	Business executives
Accountants	Entrepreneurs (owners of their own business)

Priests, ministers, rabbis

College professors, deans, presidents

College alumni, fraternity/sorority members

Community leaders, civic leaders

State and U.S. politicians

Sales personnel

Doctors, dentists, nurses

Consultants

Insurance agents

Real estate agents

Industrial managers

Stock brokers/analysts

Engineers

Friends/relatives

Artists/writers

Former supervisors/co-workers

Use this personal contact list to tell people you are in the job market and/or changing careers, to ask them for their advice, to obtain information in job fields, to learn from their successes, to obtain possible job leads, to get referrals to others who they know could be helpful to you. Figure 9–8 is a typical Personal Contact List.

Call or write these people, asking for a brief meeting. You are neither interviewing nor asking for a job; you are simply establishing a rapport and seeking information. Be sure to make this point clear to the individual when you request your meeting. Keep the meeting brief. Always send a thank-you letter to anyone who has given you time.

Instructions

Consider the following questions and approaches for getting started on your contact/information interviewing. Be prepared to ask clarifying questions.

Opinion Questions
- Is my job objective clear to you?
- What kind of work environment do you think that I would be most effective in—industrial, commercial, government, nonprofit?
- If you were in my position, what would you do?
- How did you manage your job change?
- What can I learn from your career history?
- How did you get your present position?

FIGURE 9–8

PERSONAL CONTACT LIST

NAME	TITLE	ADDRESS	PHONE

Fact Questions
- What articles, books, seminars, or educational programs are you aware of that might benefit me in my career development?
- How is your company, department, or division organized?
- Where and at what level do you think I would fit into an organization similar to this one?
- What kind of "ballpark" salary figure do you think I could command at that level?

Referral Questions
- Mr./Mrs./Ms. _____, I have learned a number of things from you during this meeting: (summarize key points). I would like to have the opportunity to talk with a number of people like yourself, who can assist me to attain my career objectives. Who do you recommend that I contact?

If there is any hesitancy, remind him/her that you will approach them in the same manner, that is, you will not be asking for a job.

Letter writing

Letter writing is an important part of your job search. Always direct a letter to a specific person, by name and title. The letter should be brief and succinct in stating your purpose. It should also be individualized and personalized to fit the situation, as well as professional in appearance.

Generally, it should not exceed one page, and it should always have a strong first sentence.

A cover letter accompanying your resume should not repeat the detailed information in your resume, but it should emphasize your skills and experience that apply to the particular position. Job campaign letters may include:

- Unsolicited cover letter
- Answering an ad letter
- Application letter
- Job acceptance/letters/ rejection letters
- Cover letter
- Thank-you letters (information interviews, persons who supplied names and leads)
- Executive recruiter letter.

Type all letters on quality printed stationery, the same stock as your resume. Have all correspondence carefully proofread.

Request for Information Meeting Letter

Dear Mr. Carr:

Mr. Charles South suggested that I contact you to obtain information in directing my career objective. I have been working in a manufacturing environment for several years and have elected manufacturing management as a career.

I do not expect you to have a position to offer me, or know of one, but any advice that you have can be very helpful to me. The enclosed resume will give you some details about my experience and background.

I will telephone you early next week to set a brief appointment convenient to your schedule.

Yours Respectfully,

Unsolicited Cover Letter

Dear Mrs. Marshall:

My current research in the food industry clearly point to ABC Corporation as a progressive leader in the field and the type of organization I would enjoy working for.

I would direct your attention to my extensive experience in food marketing outlined in the attached resume and would very much appreciate an opportunity to discuss with you how my skills and experience could be utilized by ABC Corp. My ability to create and implement new marketing strategies could be particularly useful in today's highly competitive market.

I will call your office on (five working days) to speak with you briefly on these possibilities and to arrange a meeting at your convenience.

Sincerely yours,

Referral/Approach Letter

Dear Mr. Moore:

I am writing to you at the suggestion of Mr. Smith of ABC Corporation, who strongly recommended you because of your expertise in _____ .

At this time I am seeking advice and information about my job objective (_____). I have enclosed a copy of my resume, which outlines my accomplishments and gives you some idea of my background.

Be assured, Mr. Moore, I do not expect you to have or know of a job for me. However, I believe that I could benefit from your advice and experience in my career search.

Recognizing your very busy schedule, I will call your office on (5 business days) to set an appointment any time at your convenience.

Sincerely,

Enclosure: Resume

Sample Letter to Executive Recruiter
for Position in Human Resources Management

Dear _____:

As a recruiter, you may be able to assist me in my search for new career opportunities.

My professional goal lies in the Human Resource function considering such titles as:

- Manager of Human Resource Planning
- Manager of Career Development and Planning
- Manager of Organization Planning and Development
- Manager of Human Resource Development
- Manager of Management Development and Education
- Manager of Training and Staff Development
- Internal Human Resource Management Consultant
- Senior Management Training Professional

Enclosed are resumes with professional objectives that match some of the above specific functional areas of Human Resources which demonstrate my extensive involvement and commitment to Management Development and Employee Training. My particular forte is the ability to design and develop training programs/systems as well as conduct them effectively.

I have been with _____ firms during the past years. I am willing to relocate within the U.S. with preference toward a major metropolitan area. However, the career opportunity and growth is more important than the location.

My minimum salary expectations are in the _____ and upward. Currently I am in the _____.

I would like to review Human Resource opportunities you may be aware of and you will no doubt, wish to probe more of my background. I'll call you next _____, _____, to assess any mutual interest.

Sincerely,

Enclosures

Thank-You Information Meeting Letters

Dear Ms. Smith:

Thank you for taking time to talk with me today. I am looking forward to reading the book *Developing Sales Leads* which you recommended.

I appreciate your help in thinking through my career objectives more realistically and suggesting some new directions.

I will keep you informed of my career progress.

Cordially,

Dear Mrs. Jones:

Just a note of appreciation for our meeting last Friday morning. I am grateful that you could take the time from your busy schedule to be a "sounding board" for my ideas as well as the excellent suggestions you made. I will incorporate them into my job campaign.

Thanks also for the feedback on the alumni association.

I will keep you informed of my career progress.

Yours truly,

Answering Ad Letter

Attention: Personnel Director

I am responding to your advertisement in the Morning Free Press August 20, xxxx regarding the Directorship of an urban youth employment program.

My qualifications meet your stated requirements:

Your Requirements	My Qualifications
• Develop relationships with public and private sector groups	• Six years experience lobbying in both sectors
• Staff supervision and administration	• Six years experience of staff supervision, office management and administration
• Oversee fiscal concerns	• Budget development and implementation
• Urban program development	• Helped organize Dial-A-Ride program in Mt. Pleasant, Michigan
• Private sector experience	• Three (3) years business management
• Bachelors degrees	• Bachelor of Science (Economics, Political Science)

I would appreciate a personal interview to discuss how I can contribute to the program. I have enclosed my resume for your further information.

Thank you for your consideration and I look forward to talking with you.

Sincerely,

Answering Blind Ad Letter

Box N–4705
Detroit News 48231

RE: *Ad-Shop Foreman, Detroit News, Sunday, April 13, 19XX*

I am forwarding my resume for your consideration for position as Shop Foreman.

My experience in the field of steel fabrication fits very closely with your specified needs.

I would appreciate an opportunity to discuss my qualifications with you personally and can arrange to meet with you at your convenience.

Sincerely,

Job Interview Follow-Up Letter

Dear Mrs. Black:

I enjoyed meeting with you today and I appreciate the time you took to explain the details of the marketing position in your sales department.

I am confident my background and sales experience could contribute to your current sales/marketing needs, especially since I am already familiar with the territory. Also your methods of reporting are very similar to the system I used while I was with ABC Company.

I would enjoy working with you and your staff, Ms. Black, and look forward to hearing from you in the next couple of days.

Sincerely,

Job Acceptance Letter

Dear Mr. Brown:

I am pleased to accept your offer of employment as a design engineer at your Millville plant at the annual salary of $XX,XXX.

As we discussed, I will begin on January 3, 19XX. I am looking forward to joining your staff and contributing to the design efforts of R.H. Macy Company.

Thank you for your personal help in getting the details settled.

Cordially,

Job Rejection Letter

Dear Ms. O'Connor:

Thank you for your time and the consideration you have shown me in our current job negotiations.

After much deliberation, I have decided not to accept the sales position in Denver.

I enjoyed meeting you and appreciate the professional and thorough way ABC Company works with prospective employees. It was a pleasure to meet you personally.

Cordially,

References for Further Reading

Germann, Richard and Peter Arnold. *Bernard Haldane Associates: Job & Career Building, A Step-by-Step Guide*. New York: Harper & Row, 1980.

Haldane, Bernard. *Career Satisfaction and Success*. New York: AMACOM, 1974.

Irish, Richard K. *Go Hire Yourself an Employer*. New York: Anchor Books, 1973.

10

Implementing
your marketing campaign

Job hunting is a full-time job and needs to be structured as a job: Each day must be full, scheduled, systematic, organized, directed, and action-oriented. It is unwise to begin your job search until you are ready to deal with it in this professional manner. You have spent many hours, even weeks, preparing and planning for your market campaign. Now your preparation pays off as you talk to prospective employers. A successful campaign produces results, and the results are measurable—a new job.

The cause-effect relationship of activities in a job search campaign is very clear and logically sequenced. You cannot accept a position if you do not have job offers. You do not receive offers without job interviews. You do not obtain job interviews without phoning for appointments. You do not get appointments without writing letters and sending resumes. And you cannot write letters to potential employers without leads and contacts. The relationships among these activities are diagrammed in Figure 10–1.

Chapter 9 has already assisted you in beginning these activities by developing leads and preparing written correspondence. This chapter continues to implement that process by providing direction for the latter steps of the campaign: phone calls for appointments, conducting job interviews, negotiating job offers, accepting or rejecting these offers.

Resume $\longrightarrow$ Leads $\longrightarrow$ Letters $\longrightarrow$ Phone Calls for Appointment $\longrightarrow$ Job interviews $\longrightarrow$ Job Offers $\longrightarrow$ Acceptance of New Job

FIGURE 10–1

MARKETING CAMPAIGN ACTIVITIES

EXERCISE 10–1: WEEKLY CAMPAIGN SCHEDULE

Outplaced job seekers often do not seem to accomplish as much during their campaign as they did each week when they were employed. They may have been accustomed to developing "To Do" lists each Monday morning to plan their week's work. Now, that doesn't always happen. Many job seekers have a difficult time imposing a time structure on themselves. From our experience, people who have spent 35 to 40 hours of work on their campaign each week are the most successful, simply because they met and talked with a lot of people. Therefore, we strongly urge you to set up a series of weekly goals and develop a schedule that allows you to accomplish them. The Weekly Market Campaign Schedule shown in Figures 10–2a and 10–2b can help you to get organized for your campaign.

Figures 10–3 and 10–4 contain sample entries for a typical week's activities. Your activities change during various periods during the campaign. For the first two or three weeks, more than likely you will be writing more letters than conducting interviews. Nonetheless, these figures represent a typical active week.

Let's examine these sample figures. Generally, it is not an effective practice to call to set appointments at 8:30 Monday morning when the person you want to see is probably busy scheduling his/her weeks activities. Save your phone calls for the afternoon. Do your research to develop new leads and contacts on Monday morning. Read the Sunday papers, both the want ads and the business section, to see who has been promoted or what is of current interest in the business community. Get names and addresses from articles. Conduct your information meetings and job interviews on Tuesday, Wednesday, and Thursday if possible. Try to schedule eight to nine appointments each week. Use Friday as your letter writing day, as well as for time to evaluate your campaign activities and direction. Reproduce and use the blank campaign forms to plan your weekly activities.

FIGURE 10–2a

WEEKLY MARKET CAMPAIGN SCHEDULE—AM ACTIVITIES

Week of ———— , 198———

Number of Letters ———— Number of Phone Calls ———— Number of appointments ———— Number of Job Interviews ————

Goals for Week:

	Monday, ————	Tuesday, ————	Wednesday, ————	Thursday, ————	Friday, ————
AM ACTIVITIES					

FIGURE 10–2b
WEEKLY MARKET CAMPAIGN SCHEDULE—PM ACTIVITIES

Week of _____ , 198 ____

Goals for Week: Number of Letters _____ Number of Phone Calls _____ Number of appointments _____ Number of Job Interviews _____

	Monday, _____	Tuesday, _____	Wednesday, _____	Thursday, _____	Friday, _____
PM ACTIVITIES					

FIGURE 10-3
WEEKLY MARKET CAMPAIGN SCHEDULE—AM ACTIVITIES (SAMPLE)

Week of _____ , 198___

Goals for Week: _____ Number of Letters _____ Number of Phone Calls _____ Number of appointments _____ Number of Job Interviews _____

	Monday, ___	Tuesday, ___	Wednesday, ___	Thursday, ___	Friday, ___
AM ACTIVITIES	• Read Sunday's paper for Want Ads and Business section: respond to ads. • Research Yellow Pages and Industrial Directories for leads and company information (at local library).	• Conduct job interviews and information meetings.	• Conduct job interviews and information meetings.	• Conduct job interviews and information meetings.	• Call and make appointments for next week from last Friday's letters. • Send thank-you letters from this week's interviews and meetings. • Do phone prospecting for leads.

FIGURE 10-4

WEEKLY MARKET CAMPAIGN SCHEDULE—PM ACTIVITIES (SAMPLE)

Week of _____ , 198 _____

Goals for Week: _____ Number of Letters _____ Number of Phone Calls _____ Number of appointments _____ Number of Job Interviews _____

	Monday, ____	Tuesday, ____	Wednesday, ____	Thursday, ____	Friday, ____
PM ACTIVITIES	• Phone contacts to set appointments for this week, if not reached last Friday. • Do cold call prospecting from leads in directories.	• Conduct job interviews and information meetings.	• Conduct job interviews and information meetings.	• Conduct job interviews and information meetings.	• Write letters to referrals from this week's meetings. • Send second response to Want Ads from Monday and Tuesday. • Review market campaign log for follow-up activity next week. • Plan next week's schedule and update Market Campaign Log.

TELEPHONING

The telephone is a major link between you and your potential employer. Be sure that your telephone number is clearly listed on your resume and on all correspondence, and be sure that it is a number where you can be easily reached.

Use the telephone to prospect for job leads as well as to follow up on letters, resumes, and applications submitted by mail. Follow up an interview by phone if you are interested in the job.

Avoid being interviewed on the telephone; nobody is going to hire you on the phone, but they can screen you out. Push to get a personal interview. Suggest a specific time and day, offering alternative times.

Use the Yellow Pages as a source of job search information. Review the index for the types of organizations you wish to search. By making unsolicited prospect calls, you can get the names of department heads and correct mailing address for future correspondence. You may choose to call department heads and request job interviews or information meetings. You can also request copies of the annual report in preparation for interviews.

The scripts in Figures 10–5 and 10–6 may be helpful until you are more comfortable with your own campaign telephoning style. These guidelines are only suggestions. You will quickly develop your own words and style. The first script (Figure 10–5) should be used to set appointments for meetings or interviews after you have sent a letter and resume. The person should be expecting your phone call.

The second phone script (Figure 10–6) can be used to prospect for job leads, after you have identified companies from the Yellow Pages or industrial directories. Often this method can be an efficient use of your time. An hour on the phone making 25 cold calls may result in two or three appointments, without having to wait two or three weeks for sending letters and following up.

FIGURE 10–5

Sequence of Activities	Suggested Script

If Not In:

1. "When will Mr./Ms. . . . be in so I can return the call?"
   Generally, do not leave your name and number.
   (If calling back a number of times, get the name
   of the secretary so you can identify her immediately.)

Secretary

1. Identify self:
   "This is . . ."

2. Ask for person:
   "Could I please speak
   to Mr./Ms. . . .?"

2. If you feel you are getting the runaround by the
   secretary, (a) ask her if Mr./Ms. does not wish to
   see you and then decide a course of action, (b) call
   before 8:00 A.M. or after 5:00 P.M. (5:30 P.M.), and you may
   reach the person directly.

Call Comes In

----------- -------------------------

3. If asked the nature of
   your call, "It's a
   personal matter, he/she is
   expecting my call."

If In:

1. Identify self again: "This is . . ."

2. "I wrote you recently, have you received my letter?"

3. "As I mentioned in my letter, I wrote you at the
   suggestion of . . . "

4. State purpose of meeting: "I'd like a few minutes of your
   time to obtain your suggestions about my career future."

5. Set appointment (give two options, an A.M. and P.M., two to
   three days from today). "Would Tuesday, May sixth at
   10 A.M. or Wednesday, May seventh at 4 P.M. be convenient
   for you?" (If not, negotiate.)

6. Get parking instructions and give a thank-you.

FIGURE 10–6

TELEPHONE SCRIPT FOR PROSPECTING

Sequence of Activities	Suggested Script
1. Request for name of department head for either writing letter or later phone call. 2. Hang up and redial twenty minutes later.	1. "Hello, this is _____ (name) _____ speaking; would you please tell me the name of your _____ (job title) ____ Thank you."
1. Ask secretary/receptionist for department head 2. Identify yourself to department head. 3. State purpose of call, summarize your qualifications, and ask for appointment.	1. "Hello, this is _____ (name) _____ speaking. Could I please speak with Mr./Ms. _____ 2. Mr./Ms. _____ (name) _____ This is _____ (your name) _____ speaking." 3. "Mr./Ms. _____, I'm contacting you as _____ (job title) _____ of _____ (company name) _____ to let you know my qualifications as a _____ _____ (your job objective) _____. I have _____ (summary of your qualifications) _____ I would like to speak with you in person about potential opportunities at _____ (company name) _____, now or in the future. Could we get together at your convenience on ___ (suggest two alternative dates and times) ___ _____?"
4. If yes, be sure to get correct address, directions, if necessary, parking instructions. If no, try to schedule an information meeting. 5. If no, ask for referrals. 6. If no, graciously thank person for time and hang up (gently).	4. "Mr./Ms. _____, I realize that you may not have current openings. Could I come by to meet with you to discuss possible future situations?" 5. "Mr./Ms. _____, can you suggest any other person I could contact to explore job opportunities as a _____ (your job function) _____ ?" "Mr./Ms. _____, may I use your name when I contact Mr./Ms. _____ ?" 6. "I appreciate your time. You've been most helpful. Thank you."

A person gets hired when an interviewer recognizes that:

- a candidate has ability and willingness to help the organization get a particular job done, and
- the candidate comes across as somebody with whom the interviewer would enjoy working.

Schedule two or three job interviews a day. Before each interview, get as much information about the organization as possible (from annual reports, personal contacts, directories, and the like). Details about the job, the overall industry, the particular organizations' research and development direction, their products, subsidiaries, and other information can be very helpful.

Listen to the questions that the interviewer is asking, what is behind those questions, and what problems the interviewer is saying he/she needs solved. Take a few seconds to compose your answers, and address your responses to the interviewer's needs. Where possible, tie in your accomplishments/similar experiences.

Instructions

The following sample questions are the more common ones asked by interviewers.

1. Before the interview, formulate your answers to these questions in the space provided.
2. Review your work from Chapters 3–5.
3. When you are through answering questions 1–23, think up a few questions of your own that you normally have difficulty answering.
4. Practice these questions with a spouse/friend. Practice them out loud. Hear yourself—what you are saying and how you are saying it. Attitude and enthusiasm are critical in an interview.

1. Tell me about yourself.

_____

_____

_____

_____

2. Why do you think you might like to work for us?

_____

_____

_____

_____

_____

3. How do you spend your spare time? What are your avocations and hobbies?

_____

_____

_____

_____

4. How would you evaluate your most recent boss?

_____

_____

_____

_____

5. What do you know about our company?

_____

_____

_____

_____

6. How did your previous employer treat you?

_____

_____

_____

_____

7. What type of people "rub you the wrong way?"

_____

_____

_____

_____

_____

8. What jobs have you enjoyed the most? The least? Why?

_____

_____

_____

_____

_____

9. What special abilities could you contribute to our company?

_____

_____

_____

_____

_____

10. What are your future goals?

_____

_____

_____

_____

11. How much money are you currently making?

_____

_____

_____

_____

12. What are some of your major weaknesses?

_____

_____

_____

_____

13. How do you define success?

_____

_____

_____

_____

14. How do you know that you can be successful?

_____

_____

_____

_____

_____

15. What questions to you have about us?

_____

_____

_____

_____

_____

16. Did you have any setbacks, disappointments, or things that did not turn out well? Tell me about them.

_____

_____

_____

_____

_____

_____

17. How do you think your present (past) supervisor would describe you?

_____

_____

_____

_____

18. What has contributed to your career success up to the present time?

_____

_____

_____

_____

19. This position is below your ability, isn't it?

_____

_____

_____

_____

20. You're too old (too young) for this position; we were thinking of someone about _____.

_____

_____

_____

_____

21. Why were you fired from your last job?

_____

_____

_____

22. How do you feel about being terminated by _____ company?

_____

_____

23. Are you willing to relocate or travel?

_____

_____

_____

_____

24. [Question] _____

[My response] _____

_____

_____

_____

25. [Question] _____

[My response] _____

_____

_____

_____

_____

26. [Question] _____

[My response] _____

_____

_____

_____

Tips on Interviewing

1. Be prepared to ask the interviewer questions. Ask about the job itself, about specific duties, and about your would-be boss. Why is the job available? Where does the position/department fit into the organization? Is it a high turnover position? Your homework in researching the company and its products/research/market can pay off well in this phase of the interview. You can converse with your interviewer intelligently and offer a knowledgeable, give-and-take exchange.

2. Save your questions on benefits, vacation, payday, and the like until you have a firm job offer.

3. Know when the interview is over.

4. Restate your interest in the job.

5. Determine the next move for a second interview by asking, "When should I call?" "When may I expect to hear from you?"

6. In any interviewing situation, remember that nonverbal communications play a major role. Appearance, attention, and eye contact are of utmost importance. There should be a sense of relaxed formality. Smile. It is not always the most qualified candidate who gets the position. While all hiring decisions are work-oriented, your confidence, manner, and verbal skills play a large part, and personal chemistry always comes into the process. Remember, your job is to convince the interviewer that you are the best person for the job.

7. Immediately after the interview, review what took place. How did you do? What did you feel good about? What will you do differently next time? What areas made you uncomfortable? What do you do next? Summarize and evaluate your interviews. Even what appears to be an unsuccessful interview can be useful in your campaign. Analyze your summary, and determine what you can use to improve your interviewing.

THANK-YOU LETTERS

Always follow up your interviews and contact meetings with a short thank-you letter for the person's time and consideration. This is a good opportunity to add a brief statement to reinforce some area of your experience that appeared to be of interest to the interviewer, or to mention something you feel was overlooked in the dialogue. Be *brief*.

MARKETING CAMPAIGN LOG

Many job seekers fail to realize the amount of paperwork that is necessary to implement a successful campaign. A lead is jotted down here, or a phone number is scribbled on a piece of scrap paper. After a few weeks, a feeling of chaos takes over, as people realize they need a way of organizing their information into a system. The Market Campaign Log in Figure 10–7 serves that purpose. It becomes the key source of documenting whom you wish to see, where they are located, how you can contact them, what you have sent to them, when you contacted them, what they said to you, and what you are going to do in the future as a result of this contact.

A periodic analysis of the log helps you to establish control over your campaign and gives you a direction for future activities. Are you meeting the kinds of people you need to? Are they at the right levels in the organization for you? Are you contacting the kinds of organizations you want to focus on? The log can also help you to evaluate the number of contacts and interviews you have had in a month. A comparison of the number of contacts versus the number of interviews within a month provides you with a projected goal for the next month.

Instructions

Because such a system is so critical, we recommend that you reproduce as many copies of this log as you need. Make an accurate entry of all key information in the appropriate col-

FIGURE 10-7
MARKETING CAMPAIGN LOG

Contact Name/Title	Address/Phone	Date Resume Sent	Date Phone Appt.	Summary of Meeting/Interview	Follow-Up

umns: the contact's name and title in the first column, the address and phone number of the organization in the second column, the date when you sent your resume and letter, and the date of phone call for appointment. After you have had a meeting or interview, summarize the key points in the next column. Finally, place any specific follow-up activities in the last column. To maintain order in your information system, you may wish to assign a consecutive number to each contact, placing it in the first column with the person's name.

EXERCISE 10–3: MARKET CAMPAIGN REVIEW

For greatest productivity, meet with someone who knows you well, such as a spouse, friend, fellow job seeker, career counselor, or job club. The purpose of the meeting is to review the progress of your campaign activities and to give you feedback and encouragement. Prior to meeting with this person or group, prepare for the meeting by completing the Market Campaign Review in Figure 10–8, using the data from your Market Campaign Log.

NEGOTIATING

If you are changing fields completely, you may face a reduction in compensation. There are, however, other benefits to consider, and when you are doing something you enjoy you can often recover your earning power fairly rapidly. Meanwhile, here are some tips on negotiating:

- Never accept a job before you know and agree to the entire compensation package. Take time to consider the offer.
- Include provisions for salary and performance review in your negotiating.
- Be firm, reasonable, and flexible.
- You are selling your services for 40 hours a week, and, like buying and selling any commodity, there is usually room to negotiate.
- Employee benefits, work hours, and health policies are usually set, but very often you can negotiate these features within your salary range.

FIGURE 10–8

MARKET CAMPAIGN REVIEW

1. a. Are you keeping your market campaign log up-to-date?

                                                  ____Yes ____ No

   b. Did you meet your goals for last week/month?

                                                 ____ Yes ____ No

   c. How many hours per week are you spending on your campaign?

                                               ____ Hours/Week

2. What successes have you had this week/month?

- _____

- _____

- _____

- _____

3. What problems have you encountered this week/month?

- _____

- _____

- _____

- _____

4. What can you do to solve these problems?

- _____

- _____

- _____

- _____

5. What are your job search goals for the next week/month?

_____ Number of letters and resumes to be sent

_____ Number of phone calls to be made

_____ Number of responses to want ads

Other Goals _____

_____

_____

- High salary demands do not necessarily put off an employer. If you know your worth and you are prepared to tell the employer you're worth your demands, you can convince him/her to give you what you are asking for. Know the salary range you can realistically expect.

- Never bring up the subject of salary yourself during the interview; let the interviewer introduce it. If directly queried on your salary history, you can reply in the vein, "Over the past several years it has increased at an annual rate of twelve percent. I'm sure you have considered the salary for this position. What has been budgeted for it?"

- If pushed to state your figure, first state the value of your total income package. If the reaction is decidedly negative, you can add that you are flexible and willing to negotiate. Let the interviewer know that you will consider other forms of compensation and perks/benefits that the organization may offer.

- Bargaining upward is extremely difficult, but working downward makes you look like a reasonable person. Ask for the maximum, knowing your minimum and how much you are willing to yield. Timing and judgment on when and how to discuss and negotiate salary are major factors in any successful job campaign. Listen, and be alert to money clues. If you know where you are coming from, you can trust yourself to know when to make your move.

ACCEPTING

All your efforts have paid off. You receive a job offer—or two or three! Remember, however, that the only reason you ever accept a job offer is that it is the job you want. So the right job for you may not necessarily be your first offer.

Review job offers carefully and thoroughly. You will not be expected to accept or reject a verbal offer when it is first made. If the interview does not suggest a time frame—such as, "We need your answer by Monday"—then take the initiative and ask, "When do you need my decision?" Evaluate the job, making a list of pros and cons for accepting or rejecting the position. Use the Decision Making Worksheets in Exercise

6–4. If you decide that the job is not for you but you are still tempted to accept, this is the time to trust your gut level reaction. Don't accept—there will be other offers. Once your final decision has been made, send your accept or reject letter.

Accepting a new position is not the end of the process. You are now just beginning the next step in your career development. Chapter 11 outlines some directions and steps to help you develop your new job and your career to its full potential. We strongly recommend your working through this chapter immediately after accepting your new job.

References for Further Reading

Azrin, Nathan A. and Victoria A. Besalel. *Job Club Counselor's Manual.* Baltimore Md.: University Park Press, 1980.

Cohen, William A. *The Executive's Guide to Finding a Superior Job.* New York: AMACOM, 1978.

Lathrop, Richard. *Who's Hiring Who?* Reston, Va.: Reston Publishing Co., 1976.

11

Starting your next job on the right foot

Before you actually begin your new job, spend some time mentally preparing yourself for this next step in your career. The following action steps ensure that you are off to a positive start:

- Send announcement and appreciation letters to significant contacts
- Maintain the Weekly Achievement Log
- Set short-term career goals
- Learn how to "manage" your boss
- Prepare for your first performance review

SENDING LETTERS TO SIGNIFICANT CONTACTS

Since many people have taken an interest in your market campaign, they would probably like to know the results. If you have had an extensive campaign, you may not be able to write each person a letter. Review your Market Campaign Log, and identify the people who were your significant contacts. Write letters to them, announcing your new position and again expressing your appreciation and gratitude for the personal time and effort they expended on your behalf.

People appreciate thank-you letters. It validates them and builds their self-esteem. It also informs them of your whereabouts if they wish to contact you in the near future. Include your new business card if you have one.

Remember, your career is built in the future, often by your own public relations and marketing efforts. The more often people hear about your career, the better for you. This may not be the last time in your career that you need your contact's assistance. Who's to say that you won't be looking for another job sometime in the future. From anyone's perspective, it's always good to receive "appreciation" letters as well as "need" letters.

WEEKLY LOG OF ACHIEVEMENTS

An ongoing task for your future is logging a weekly record of your work achievements. This is an excellent time to begin this helpful practice. The weekly log is a way of controlling your future career. By recording achievements, you discover patterns in your work life. This is a continuation of your career progression analysis (Figure 4–6). Use a notebook or duplicate the Weekly Achievement Log (Figure 11–1), and add the new pages to this workbook. After a few months, you have a precise "replay" of your career in action.

Why keep the log? First, it becomes a valuable asset when preparing for your periodic performance review. You see not just the work that was assigned and completed, but also any additional responsibilities. The log should also include notations on reasons why some assignments were late or went awry. This data gives you a more insightful review of your own performance. By entering data weekly, it is easier to remember what you accomplished than trying to recall details six or twelve months later.

The second reason for logging achievements is that the information provides you with up-to-date career information that you can use to update your resume. Being serious about your career development, you should always have a current resume. You never know when someone may ask for a copy, and it's embarrassing to admit that recent accomplishments or publications are not included. A good practice is to revise and update your resume every six months. A resume is a verbal

FIGURE 11–1

Week of	Achievement	Significant Notations

picture of your career potential at any one point in time. As you change, learn new skills, and develop increased competencies, your resume should indicate these changes. The weekly log gives you the raw data for these revisions. You should never have to start from scratch again as you did in this workbook.

EXERCISE 11–1: SETTING SHORT-TERM CAREER GOALS

Another reason for maintaining a career diary is for a periodic career audit and goal-setting session. This may coincide with rewriting your resume. Reread all your achievement incidents and begin to analyze them, using the Career Audit Summary Sheet (Figure 11–2). The purposes of the Career Audit are to summarize the date you recorded in your weekly log and to give you a picture of your overall career activities so you can effectively manage your future. It should take you about 20–30 minutes to complete the audit.

FIGURE 11–2
CAREER AUDIT SUMMARY

1. Date _____ 2. For 6 month period ending _____
3. Number of achievements during 6 month period _____
4. Who was involved in the achievement incident?
5. How or where were you involved in accomplishing the achievement?

	No. of Incidents	% of Time		No. of Incidents	% of Time
• Superior	_____	____	• Writing	_____	____
• Peers	_____	____	• Reflecting	_____	____
• Subordinates	_____	____	• Reading	_____	____
• Alone	_____	____	• Social	_____	____
• External contacts	_____	____	• Telephone	_____	____
• Other internal employees	_____	____	• Formal meeting	_____	____
			• Informal meeting	_____	____
• Other	_____	____	• Other	_____	____
Total	_____	100%	Total	_____	100%

Adapted from T. Bonama and D. Slevins Time Management exercise in their *Executive Survival Manual*.

FIGURE 11-2
(Cont.)

6. What organizational areas were your achievements?

	No. of Incidents	% of Time
• Marketing/sales	_____	____
• Operations/ Production	_____	____
• Accounting/ Finance	_____	____
• Human Resources/ Personnel	_____	____
• Training and development	_____	____
• Research and Development	_____	____
• Public relations	_____	____
• Engineering	_____	____
• Data processing	_____	____
• Administration/ general management	_____	____
• Other	_____	____
Total	_____	100%

7. What aspect of your job function were you doing?

	No. of Incidents	% of Time
• Planning	_____	____
• Organizing	_____	____
• Directing/ Controlling	_____	____
• Coordinating	_____	____
• Delegating	_____	____
• Staffing	_____	____
• Reporting	_____	____
• Budgeting	_____	____
• Researching	_____	____
• Communicating	_____	____
• Motivating	_____	____
• Creating/designing	_____	____
• Instructing	_____	____
• Other	_____	____
Total	_____	100%

	Yes	No
8. • Are you personally satisfied with the number of achievements during the six-month period?	[ ]	[ ]
• Are you happy with the location of the achievements in the sub-categories of question 4–7?	[ ]	[ ]
• Have you accomplished what you set out to do?	[ ]	[ ]

- Would you like to change your time allocations in the next six months in terms of the following categories:

	Yes	No
● Who is involved in the achievement	[ ]	[ ]
● How or where you accomplish it	[ ]	[ ]
● The organizational area	[ ]	[ ]
● The job function area	[ ]	[ ]

- Every yes response requires an action plan on your part, as well as a stronger indication of personal career management.

9. Of all the achievements, which one was the most effective incident—that is, the one that had the highest quality of work performance?

_____

_____

_____

10. Which achievement would be least effective? _____

_____

_____

_____

11. In reviewing your responses to questions 4–7, which areas would you like to spend *more* time on during the next six months?

_____

_____

_____

_____

12. Which items do you want to spend *less* time on? _____

_____

_____

_____

FIGURE 11–2
(Cont.)

13. What are your short-term career goals for the next six months?

a. _____

_____

b. _____

_____

c. _____

_____

d. _____

_____

_____

14. What are some strategies to achieve these goals? How are you going to accomplish them?

a. Do nothing (or do nothing differently)!

b. _____

_____

_____

c. _____

_____

_____

d. _____

_____

_____

e. "Surprise Option" (Innovative/Creative) _____

_____

_____

_____

_____

EXERCISE 11–2: ASSESSING ORGANIZATION CLIMATE

Another way for you to set your career goals is to study the organizational chart of your department. One of the first things you should ask for on the new job is a copy of the department organizational chart. It is important to study the "paper" chart so that you understand the major personalities and organizational climate of your department. After you have been in your new position six to twelve weeks, you should begin to chart the "real" organizational structure. In most companies, there is a difference between the real and paper charts. It is critical that you learn early to deal with the political relationships of the organization. Begin by observing relationships, how people talk to you, and how they talk to one another.

Instructions

To assess the organizational climate, draw the real chart as you perceive it, asking yourself the following questions to understand your boss and his/her environmental context, your peers' needs and situations, as well as your own position.

- What are my boss's organizational goals?
- What are his/her personal career goals?
- What are pressures placed on him/her from superiors and peers?
- What are my peers' organizational goals?
- What are their personal goals?
- What pressures do they have on them? From whom?
- What kinds of conflicts have surfaced?
- What kinds of misunderstandings are there?
- Who really has the power in this department?
- What kinds of power are used?
- What are the inevitable problems?
- How are they solved?

After analyzing your situation with these questions, draw the "real" organizational chart and compare it to the department's "paper" chart (Figure 11–3).

FIGURE 11–3
COMPARING ORGANIZATIONAL CHARTS

Paper Organizational Chart

Real Organizational Chart

EXERCISE 11–3: DEALING WITH EXPECTATIONS

After viewing your perception of how your department operates, you may find that you are experiencing role conflict. Your boss, your peers, your subordinates, and you yourself may all have different expectations. For example, in a true-to-life situation, the boss's goal was to improve profits, and the subordinates' goal was to regain market share. After two quarters of declining margins and continued deterioration of the financial situation, the new vice president of marketing was fired. Dealing with four different levels of expectancies, you often experience conflicts and have to manage these ambiguities.

Instructions

Identify the four different sets of expectations in Figure 11–4. Then resolve any conflicts by working through the worksheet in Figure 11–5.

FIGURE 11–4
FOUR DIFFERENT SETS OF EXPECTATIONS

My view of my role as: _____[Position]

- _____
- _____
- _____
- _____
- _____

How my boss sees my role:

- _____
- _____
- _____
- _____
- _____

The expectations my peers have of me:

- _____
- _____
- _____
- _____
- _____

What my subordinates expect of me:

- _____
- _____
- _____
- _____
- _____

FIGURE 11–5

ROLE CONFLICT RESOLUTIONS

The major set of role
conflicts are

[ ] Between my boss's
expectations and my own
[ ] Between my boss's expectations and my subordinates
[ ] Between my boss's expectations and my peers

(Check the appropriate
boxes):

[ ] Between my peers'
expectations and my own
[ ] Between my subordinates'
expectations and my own
[ ] Between my peers' expectations and my subordinates

Conflicts that *must* be resolved:

Conflict	How?	When?

Conflicts and role ambiguities that I can live with:

_____

_____

_____

_____

_____

Conflicts that I don't have to resolve:

_____

_____

_____

_____

_____

The most important career relationship is between you and your boss. Your career advancement or even survival depends largely on the effectiveness of this relationship. Most of us know of talented and aggressive managers who actively supervise subordinates, products, markets and technology, but who take a passive, almost ignoring, role of their bosses and find themselves plateaued or fired.

For many people the phrase "Managing Your Boss" sounds suspicious or unusual. We are referring not to political maneuvering or apple polishing, but rather to the concept of managing a compatible relationship with your supervisor. Spending time and energy consciously working with your boss to obtain the best results for you is critical to managing your career effectively.

Recognize that your relationship with your boss involves mutual dependence between two fallible human beings. Your boss relies on your help and cooperation to do his/her job effectively. In turn, you need help and information from the boss to perform your job well. The boss is your critical link to the rest of the organization.

To assume that you can operate with complete self-sufficiency is counter-productive to your future. Therefore, if you are going to have a relationship of mutual dependence, you must be aware of and have an understanding of your boss's strengths, weaknesses, work styles, values, and goals.

Instructions

Having completed Chapters 3–5, you have a working understanding of your own strengths, limitations, goals, values, and preferred work styles. The exercise in Figure 11–6 provides you with the information you need to develop and manage a healthy working relationship between you and your boss.

The purpose of this exercise was to sensitize you to your boss's work style. Once you become aware of that person's strengths and limitations, you can complement this relationship by compensating for his/her limitations and capitalizing on his/her strengths. Your boss is half of the relationship. You are the other half, and you have direct control over that half of the relationship—your own behavior.

FIGURE 11–6
EFFECTIVELY MANAGING UPWARD

1. Prepare an assessment of your boss' major strengths and
   weaknesses.

   Strengths   Weaknesses

   - _____   - _____
   - _____   - _____
   - _____   - _____
   - _____   - _____
   - _____   - _____

2. What are your boss's major professional career goals?

   - _____
   - _____
   - _____
   - _____
   - _____

3. How does he/she clarify them for you?

   - _____
   - _____
   - _____
   - _____
   - _____

4. How do you compensate for your boss's limitations and
   weaknesses?

   - _____
   - _____
   - _____
   - _____

FIGURE 11–6
(Cont.)

5. How do you clarify your boss's expectations of you?

- _____
- _____
- _____
- _____

6. What pressures are placed on your boss by his/her boss and his/her peers?

- _____
- _____
- _____
- _____

7. What information do you need from your boss to perform your job well? How do you get it?

- _____
- _____
- _____
- _____

8. How and when do you communicate your expectations to your boss?

How?	When?

- _____
- _____
- _____
- _____

FIGURE 11–6
(Cont.)

9. How do you communicate problems, failures, the "bad news" to your boss?

- _____
- _____
- _____
- _____

Check the appropriate column for each question.

	Yes	No	
10.	___	___	Do you assume primary responsibility for your own career and professional development?
11.	___	___	Do you know and understand your boss's needs and preferred work style?
12.	___	___	Does your boss thrive on conflict?
13.	___	___	Does your boss minimize conflict?
14.	___	___	Does your boss prefer to receive information in memos?
15.	___	___	Does your boss prefer to receive information through phone calls?
16.	___	___	Does your boss like formal meetings?
17.	___	___	Do you assume it's your boss's responsibility to develop your career?
18.	___	___	Is your boss a listener?
19.	___	___	Is your boss a reader?
20.	___	___	Is your boss's decision-making style "high involvement?"
21.	___	___	Does your boss prefer a "delegating" decision-making style?"
22.	___	___	Is your working relationship with your boss compatible?

23. What did you learn from this experience on managing the boss-subordinate relationship?

● _____

● _____

● _____

● _____

24. What do you want to do about that relationship in the future?

● _____

● _____

● _____

● _____

The energy it takes to manage this relationship may be unequal. In fact, you may indeed have to spend more time and energy at it than your boss. If you analyze how you use your relationship time on the job, it may look like the diagram in Figure 11–7. For simplicity sake, we have divided the square into equal quarters. In reality the percentages may be slightly different in your situation. We're assuming that you direct 25 percent of your time and energy to yourself and to personal job activities. Another 25 percent of your energy is directed to your boss and managing this relationship. We also assume that another 25 percent of your energy is directed to the interaction with your peers. Lastly, 25 percent of your time is directed toward the affairs of your subordinates.

When you look at how your boss spends his/her time and energy, more than likely the percentage breakdowns are about the same as yours with the diagram looking as it does in Figure 11–8. Your boss directs about 25 percent of his/her time and energy to self and personal aspects of the job. Another 25

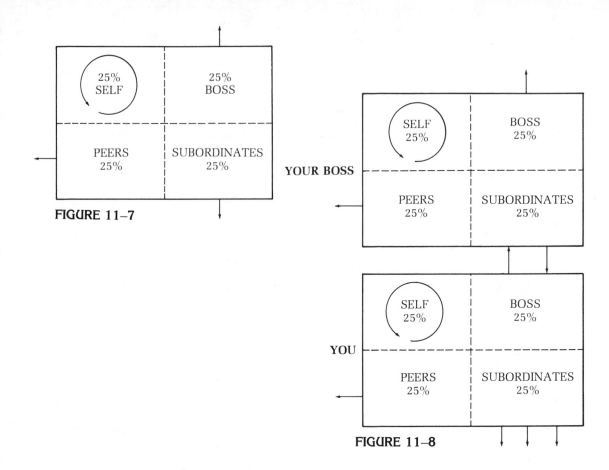

FIGURE 11–7

YOUR BOSS

YOU

FIGURE 11–8

percent of his/her energy is directed upward to his/her boss and managing this relationship. We can also assume that another 25 percent is directed to the interactions with peers in the organization. Lastly, 25 percent is directed toward subordinates.

The amount of energy and time directed to you will only be the same as you channel to your boss if you are the only subordinate. In most cases, that is not true. Your boss may have to split his/her time and energy three ways, ten ways, or more ways, depending on the number of subordinates.

The upward-downward management relationship is shown in Figure 11–9. It does not take much mathematics to realize that there is usually a disproportionate relationship between you and your boss in terms of time and energy. You generally have more time and energy available to direct "upward" in this management relationship than your boss has to direct "downward." In fact, you may have to direct upward

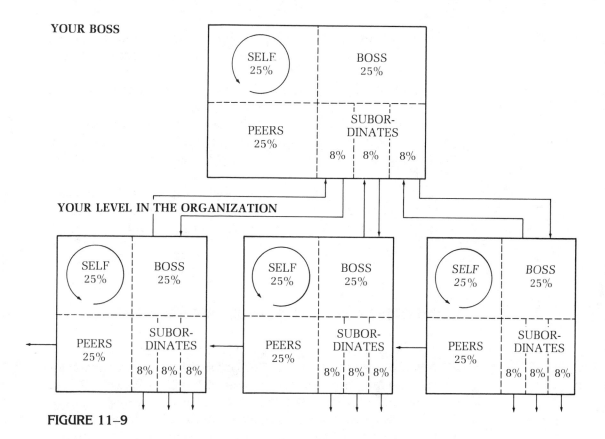

YOUR BOSS

SELF 25%	BOSS 25%
PEERS 25%	SUBOR- DINATES
	8% 8% 8%

YOUR LEVEL IN THE ORGANIZATION

SELF 25%	BOSS 25%
PEERS 25%	SUBOR- DINATES
	8% 8% 8%

SELF 25%	BOSS 25%
PEERS 25%	SUBOR- DINATES
	8% 8% 8%

SELF 25%	BOSS 25%
PEERS 25%	SUBOR- DINATES
	8% 8% 8%

FIGURE 11–9

two to three times more effort than is reciprocated. Once you know your boss's style, you must channel and direct your energy in a manner that optimizes this relationship. What are the things that you do, or can do, to improve and build this upward relationship?

A key factor in this relationship is your method of communication. How often do you talk with your boss? If you talk to your boss only once a week, you should make opportunities to change that to two or three times a week. What is your preferred communication style? If your style is a direct "telling" to the boss, you may want to adopt a "consultative" style, presenting alternatives and asking your boss for advice on what he/she considers to be the optimal solution. What issues do you talk about? Do you try to get to know him/her on a personal basis? Do you ever take him/her out for lunch? Make sure you keep your boss informed on your work activities. Don't wait for your annual performance review to fill him/her in. Don't underestimate what he/she needs to know, and make sure you find ways to keep him/her informed through a process that fits his/her work style.

Your boss has only so much time and resources available for you. Every request you make to him/her uses up some of these resources. Don't waste the boss's time over relatively trivial issues and make it difficult for him/her to meet more important goals. Use common sense to selectively utilize these resources.

Your future career in an organization depends on many factors. The most critical is your boss. The time and energy you spend in managing that relationship becomes an investment in your future.

PREPARING FOR YOUR PERFORMANCE REVIEW

Performance reviews constitute a valuable career tool. They can result in increased responsibilities, promotions, advancements, and salary increases, as well as being the best on-the-job learning situations that you may have.

Your review meeting is more productive if your prepare for it. Know when the review will take place and what is going to be assessed. Prior to the review, both you and your boss should agree on what your expected performance will be. It's best to have this in writing. Your review is then an evaluation of the progress of your short- and long-term goals. Your personal preparation should include completion of the weekly logs and career audit sheet. Bring them to the meeting so that you have this data readily available.

View your boss as a counselor rather than as a judge or prosecuting attorney. He/she has an investment in you and wants you to do well. If you don't look good, he/she isn't going to look good during his/her reviews.

You are learning from your past performance to set goals for future performance. When your boss makes general statements, ask him/her to be specific. If you are falling short of your performance expectation levels, ask your boss for suggestions on ways to meet them, along with definite target dates for your improvement. Finally, get your evaluation in writing before you sign it. Never sign a blank review form.

References for Further Reading

Bonoma, Thomas V. and Dennis P. Slevin. *Executive Survival Manual*. Boston, Mass.: CBI Publishing Company, 1978.

Cotter, John P. and John J. Gabarro. "Managing Your Boss," *Harvard Business Review* (January–February 1980), pp. 92–100.

Odiorne, George S. *Personal Effectiveness*. Westfield, Mass.: MBO, Inc., 1979.

Oliver, Robert. *Career Unrest: A Source of Creativity*. New York: Columbia University, Center for Research in Career Development, 1981.

Sweeny, Neil R. *The Art of Managing Managers*. Reading, Mass.: Addison-Wesley Publishing Company, 1981.

Index